# Cambridge Elements

Elements of Christianity and Science
edited by
Andrew Davison
*University of Cambridge*

# SCIENCE FICTION AND CHRISTIAN THEOLOGY

Victoria Lorrimar
*University of Notre Dame in Australia*

Shaftesbury Road, Cambridge CB2 8EA, United Kingdom

One Liberty Plaza, 20th Floor, New York, NY 10006, USA

477 Williamstown Road, Port Melbourne, VIC 3207, Australia

314–321, 3rd Floor, Plot 3, Splendor Forum, Jasola District Centre, New Delhi – 110025, India

103 Penang Road, #05–06/07, Visioncrest Commercial, Singapore 238467

Cambridge University Press is part of Cambridge University Press & Assessment, a department of the University of Cambridge.

We share the University's mission to contribute to society through the pursuit of education, learning and research at the highest international levels of excellence.

www.cambridge.org
Information on this title: www.cambridge.org/9781009565585

DOI: 10.1017/9781009428880

© Victoria Lorrimar 2025

This publication is in copyright. Subject to statutory exception and to the provisions of relevant collective licensing agreements, no reproduction of any part may take place without the written permission of Cambridge University Press & Assessment.

When citing this work, please include a reference to the DOI 10.1017/9781009428880

First published 2025

*A catalogue record for this publication is available from the British Library*

ISBN 978-1-009-56558-5 Hardback
ISBN 978-1-009-42891-0 Paperback
ISSN 2634-3460 (online)
ISSN 2634-3452 (print)

Cambridge University Press & Assessment has no responsibility for the persistence or accuracy of URLs for external or third-party internet websites referred to in this publication and does not guarantee that any content on such websites is, or will remain, accurate or appropriate.

For EU product safety concerns, contact us at Calle de José Abascal, 56, 1°, 28003 Madrid, Spain, or email eugpsr@cambridge.org

# Science Fiction and Christian Theology

Elements of Christianity and Science

DOI: 10.1017/9781009428880
First published online: May 2025

Victoria Lorrimar
*University of Notre Dame in Australia*

**Author for correspondence:** Victoria Lorrimar, victoria.lorrimar@nd.edu.au

**Abstract:** Theologians often struggle to engage with scientific and technological proposals meaningfully in our contemporary context. This Element provides an introduction to the use of science fiction as a conversation partner for theological reflection, arguing that it shifts the science – religion dialogue away from propositional discourse in a more fruitful and imaginative direction. Science fiction is presented as a mediator between theological and scientific disciplines and worldviews in the context of recent methodological debates. Several sections provide examples of theological engagement in relation to the themes of embodiment, human uniqueness, disability and economic inequalities, exploring relevant technologies such as mind-uploading, artificial intelligence, and virtual reality in dialogue with select works of science fiction. A final section considers the pragmatic challenge of progress in the real world towards the more utopian futures presented in science fiction.

**Keywords:** science fiction, science and religion, embodiment, mind-uploading, virtual reality, artificial intelligence

© Victoria Lorrimar 2025

ISBNs: 9781009565585 (HB), 9781009428910 (PB), 9781009428880 (OC)
ISSNs: 2634-3460 (online), 2634-3452 (print)

# Contents

1  Introduction: The Genre of Science Fiction                1
2  Science Fiction as Mediator                               7
3  Embodiment                                               14
4  Human Uniqueness                                         32
5  Disability, Economic Inequality, and Access              43
6  Conclusion: 'Staying with the Trouble' and Christian Hope  59

   References                                               63

# 1 Introduction: The Genre of Science Fiction

Many academics are probably familiar with the challenge of trying to explain what they do for a living in casual encounters with other people. 'I study religion and the ways people make sense of their lives and/or look for meaning and fulfillment' sounds pretty grandiose and abstract. But whenever I have mentioned that I am interested in the way technology is shaping and revealing our understanding of what it means to be human, I have almost always received the same response. People are more enthusiastic than confused (or bored!), and almost inevitably reference a recent or classic science fiction example (*Bladerunner*, *Black Mirror*, *Gattaca*, etc.).

Science fiction seems to be a helpful way into discussing many of the questions that emerging technologies are drawing our attention to, evergreen questions about human being and purpose and what we think the future might look like. This Element considers some of the ways that Christian theology in particular might intersect with themes explored in science fiction, and benefit from using science fiction in theological reflection, construction, and illustration.

We might argue that many of the themes so prevalent in science fiction *are* religious themes. As David Seed asks, 'The presence of religion in science fiction is hardly surprising given its tendency to question limits and boundaries, and what could be more challenging than the limitation of mortality itself?'[1] Science fiction is a rich source for illuminating the narratives that inform our understanding of human being and future hope, and examinations of science fiction trajectories have revealed a more accepting stance towards religion alongside science and technology in the contemporary imagination.[2]

This Element begins with some methodological considerations. Section 1 introduces science fiction as a genre, defining some of its shared characteristics and exploring the ways in which science fiction is related to reality. Section 2 turns to the specific place of science fiction in the intersection of science and religion, situating engagement with science fiction within the broader methodological context of the field.

The remaining sections of this Element present specific examples of how science fiction can provide alternative perspectives for our theological imagination. Each of these sections begins with an issue that is affecting our broader culture and shows up in some of our dominant theological perspectives as

---

[1] Seed (2011, 123).
[2] Hrotic (2016).

well, then draws on select works of science fiction and alternative theological frameworks as conversation partners to chart a better course. Section 3 focuses on embodiment, considering the visions of mind uploading and the technological Singularity that permeate aspects of transhumanist discourse and are well-represented in science fiction. The implications for a theological understanding of embodiment will be explored against the context of gnosticism and resurrection theologies. Section 4 highlights the decentring of the human in the fictional works of Becky Chambers, as part of a theological reflection on human uniqueness and the significance of humans among the creation. Section 5 engages fictional representations of virtual realities in relation to access, exploring questions around disability and economic inequalities in accessing emerging technologies. A concluding section considers some of the ongoing challenges, especially around converting imagination into practical action.

There is much discussion of specific technologies in the pages to come – artificial intelligence, brain–machine interfaces, mind-uploading, and more. For the purposes of this work, the actual scientific feasibility of such technologies is the least interesting thing about them, and will not be discussed. The focus will be on how *imagining* such technologies affects our thinking about theology, philosophy, culture, politics and more, particularly through encountering them in science fiction. The theological concepts discussed are also necessarily incomplete – the goal is to demonstrate how drawing on fiction opens up questions for robust theological reflection and engagement with contemporary concerns, rather than the systematisation of theological conclusions.

Science fiction incorporates various media, including films, graphic novels and games. This Element will focus mainly on works of print fiction for reasons of both personal preference/familiarity and limitations of scope. I also focus intentionally on science fiction texts that do not explicitly reference a Christian faith in their imagined worlds, not because such works are not valuable, but because I wish to show the value of science fiction more generally (using examples that have a wider audience). In some of the works cited, religion is peripheral; in others there are fictional religious movements that bear varying degrees of resemblance to existing religious traditions. In keeping with the aforementioned claim, the major themes we see in many science fiction works are inherently religious in nature, and regardless of the specific portrayal of (or absence of) religion in individual science fiction texts, the imagined technologies and their social, economic, and political implications provide much food for Christian theological thought.

## 1.1 What Is Science Fiction?

According to Brian Willems, science fiction 'can imagine true alternatives to our present, which is mired in the human-created oppression of people, the environment, and other living beings'.[3] Science fiction aficionados often make bold claims for its scope and impact such as this, so it is worth thinking about what makes a particular work of fiction 'science fiction'.

When it comes to definitions, however, they are legion. There seems to be little consensus as to how exactly we classify science fiction, although most attempts tend to highlight futuristic and technological elements. Though broad, science fiction author Nalo Hopkinson's description of the genre as 'the literatures that explore the fact that we are tool-makers and users, and are always changing our environment' is as good as any we might find.[4]

Authors and readers of science fiction often distinguish between 'hard' science fiction, which places great emphasis on the details and mechanisms of the hypothetical technologies represented, and 'soft' science fiction, which is less concerned with the technology itself and more interested in the social, political, religious, and/or economic context in which the technology is situated. Robert Heinlein's claim that speculative fiction is generally either about people or about gadgets is apt here.[5]

Science fiction is often grouped together with fantasy under the umbrella term of 'speculative fiction', highlighting the similarities between the genres in terms of world-building. The present work distinguishes science fiction within the broader speculative fiction category in alignment with Judith Merril's contention that science fiction in particular:

> ...makes use of the traditional 'scientific method' (observation, hypothesis, experimentation) to examine some postulated approximation of reality, by introducing a given set of changes – imaginary or inventive – into the common background of 'known facts,' creating an environment in which the responses and perceptions of the characters will reveal something about the inventions, the characters, or both.[6]

## 1.2 Science Fiction and Reality

Science fiction generally sets out to interrogate real-world social, technological, political, biological phenomena, and so on and to explore possible

---

[3] Willems (2020, 200).
[4] Hopkinson (2003, 144–145).
[5] Heinlein (2017, 17).
[6] Merril (2017, 26).

alternatives and their ramifications. Enrico Terrone identifies a common underlying structure between science fiction and philosophical thought experiments.[7] Similarly, David Seed describes a science fiction narrative as 'an embodied thought experiment whereby aspects of our familiar reality are transformed or suspended.'[8]

As Cory Doctorow highlights, even though we tend to associate science fiction with the future, the most memorable science fiction stories captivate the public imagination through what they tell us about the present.[9] Sherryl Vint also emphasises this contemporary aspect of science fiction – while it is often situated in the future, it examines the anxiety we currently feel about that future.[10] Science fiction offers us an 'imagined sense of what tomorrow's forms of life might look like' and thus is a particular kind of 'truth-telling', assert Clark Miller and Ira Bennett, who argue that the genre should play a more significant role in the assessment of putative technologies.[11]

Indeed, many authors and critics highlight the contribution of science fiction in evaluating the potential consequences of technologies, or even preparing us for their inevitability. Science fiction writer Samuel R. Delaney frames science fiction as 'training for thinking about the actual changes – sometimes catastrophic, often confusing – that the real world funnels at us year after year'.[12] Le Guin describes the future as 'a safe, sterile laboratory for trying out ideas in, a means of thinking about reality' that science fiction capitalises upon.[13] Philosopher of technology Jacques Ellul's reflections take on a more sinister nature, with the suggestion that science fiction's depiction of extreme uses of technology actually serves to make us complacent in response to present anxieties.[14] 'We take refuge in the real technological society in order to escape the fiction that was presented as the true technology.'[15]

Science fiction can reflect reality beyond a narrow perspective on specific technologies. The relationship between art and truth has been well traversed, but science fiction in particular is well equipped to convey certain truths about the human condition. The essential gesture of science fiction, according to Le Guin is 'the pulling back from "reality" in order to see it better.'[16] The next

---

[7] Terrone (2021, 27).
[8] Seed (2011, 2).
[9] Doctorow (2017, 209).
[10] Vint (2007, 22).
[11] Miller and Bennett (2008, 604).
[12] As quoted in Gunn (May 2014).
[13] As quoted in Gunn (May 2014).
[14] Ellul (1980, 112).
[15] Ellul (1980, 112).
[16] Le Guin (1973, 43–44).

section will give more consideration to how this capacity is relevant for the field of science and religion.

Science fiction not only explores hypothetical technologies and their associated social contexts, however. It also inspires the real-world *development* of certain technologies.[17] Examples are plentiful – perhaps the most cited is the handheld communication device from the original *Star Trek* series as the inspiration behind the invention of the mobile phone in the 1970s.[18] Many writers of science fiction have been recognised scientists at the same time, for example, Geoffrey Landis, Arthur C. Clarke, and Charles Sheffield.[19] Marc Pesce contends that science fiction has been '*the* deciding influence on the direction of software development'.[20] Without exaggerating the degree of influence, there is an imaginative feedback loop at play between science and science fiction, even if some scientists take pains to deny any cultural influences on their work.[21]

Serious scientific scholarship at times draws on science fiction for illustrative or inspirational purposes.[22] Science fiction can also forge connections between popular science works, which share much in common with some forms of science fiction, and funding awarded to prospective scientific research. Robert Geraci describes this link particularly in the context of apocalyptic AI narratives:

> The value of the apocalyptic imagination lies in its power to create excitement in the lay public and government funding agencies. Pop science in general, and Apocalyptic AI in particular, is a – sometimes conscious, sometimes unconscious – strategy for the acquisition of cultural prestige, especially as such prestige is measured in financial support.[23]

It is clear, then, that science fiction is far more influential in our scientific and technological economy than is sometimes credited. And while science fiction is most often recognised as a medium of science communication, it can communicate historical, political, philosophical and theological ideas just as well.

---

[17] See for example Bly (2005); Brake and Hook (2008); Disch (1998); Shatner and Walter (2002).
[18] Davies (27 April 2016).
[19] Science fiction authored by scientists is common enough that at least one anthology has been published (Brotherton (2017)).
[20] Pesce (October 1999).
[21] Milburn (2010, 263).
[22] Milburn (2014, 529).
[23] Geraci (2010, 3).

## 1.3 Why Does (Science) Fiction Matter?

Finally we turn to this broader appeal and influence of science fiction beyond scientific and technological environments. Literature scholar Emelie Jonsson hypothesises that the human imagination serves an adaptive function from an evolutionary perspective, allowing us to construct virtual worlds in which we gain experiences that shape our decisions and actions and the meaning we make of them in the real world.[24]

Mary Wollstonecraft Shelley's *Frankenstein* (1818) is perhaps the paradigmatic example of science fiction, helpful for thinking through the purpose and scope of the genre. It exemplifies the timelessness of some of the central questions tackled by many works of science fiction.[25] What does it mean to be human? What responsibilities do we have for and towards our creations? Are there limits to human creativity? It considers how moral understanding requires development, and challenges us on how we determine whether a being is a person.[26] Concerning the ongoing relevance of Shelley's novel to how we think about science and technology, J.M. van der Laan writes that

> …the meditative thinking of literature as exemplified in *Frankenstein* offers an alternative and counterbalance, maybe even an antidote, to the calculative thinking of science and technology, possibly even a rescue from its dangers.[27]

The enduring popularity of *Frankenstein* resonates with Mark Johnson's account of how fictional narratives 'provide us rich, humanly realistic experimental settings in which we can make our own moral explorations'.[28] While van der Laan contrasts the meditative mode of the novel with the calculation of science and technology in the quote earlier, this does not amount to a rejection of what science and technology have to offer. Instead, the scope of fiction invites us to consider broader questions that might otherwise be sidelined or ignored in the everyday work of scientists and technologists. The questions explored in the novel are universal, existential ones, and therefore occupy a great deal of theological and philosophical thinking as well.

Is there a practical benefit to the kind of philosophical reflection that science fiction can facilitate? The value of fiction in all genres for moral formation has been identified in several contexts. Scholar of medical ethics P. Anne Scott argues that the 'serious reading of literature' can nurture the imagination for

---

[24] Jonsson (2021, 22–25).
[25] Maienschein and MacCord (2017).
[26] Maienschein and MacCord (2017, 220–221).
[27] van der Laan (2010, 303).
[28] M. Johnson (1993, 198).

the proper practice of medicine, and recommends this be built into medical training.[29] Martha Nussbaum describes how the narrative and emotional structures of novels function as 'forms of Aristotelian ethical thinking' that illuminate our understanding of the good.[30] The impact of narrative and story on how people act in the world is an ongoing question to be explored throughout the rest of this work.

In a discussion of the 'purpose' of fiction, however, it would be wrong to speak of it only in terms of its value for prompting reflection about existential and/or moral concerns. While this work will focus on how science fiction can contribute to theological reflection, it is premised on a firm commitment to the pleasure and benefit of reading for its own sake.[31]

## 2 Science Fiction as Mediator

Beginning with the premise that reading fiction is worthwhile for its own sake, this section considers how science fiction in particular can be incorporated into scholarly work in the field of science and religion. It will begin with a brief discussion of methodological approaches within the field of science and religion (focusing on Christian theology to align with this Elements series) to set the scene for how science fiction might fit into trajectories within science and religion scholarship.

### 2.1 Methodology in Science and Religion

It was less than two decades ago that Taede Smedes declared the science and religion field had reached a 'mid-life crisis'.[32] Scholars of science and religion were mainly engaged in internal dialogue, Smedes argued, with neither scientists nor theologians outside the discipline registering much interest in that dialogue. According to Smedes, science and religion had become dominated by a cultural scientism that was essentially baked into the field's origins by its scientist founders, and this logic of apportioning heuristic priority to the sciences had locked science and religion scholarship into a near hopeless trajectory.[33]

---

[29] Scott (1997, 49).
[30] Nussbaum (1990, 390–391).
[31] This qualification warrants explicit affirmation given the historical tendency in certain Christian traditions to discourage reading for entertainment alone. Such a tendency is illustrated effectively by the pompous and pious clergyman Mr Collins, in Jane Austen's *Pride and Prejudice*, who is dismayed when presented with a novel to read aloud, protesting that he never reads novels and selecting instead a collection of sermons.
[32] Smedes (2008, 236).
[33] Smedes (2008).

Smedes' assessment highlights the long running science-religion dialogue on the topic of divine action as an exemplar of the theological naturalism that apparently pervades the field. Instead of seeking grand unifying theories between science and religion, Smedes advises that the way out of this stagnation is to focus on reaching understanding between scientists and theologians at smaller scales, increasing cross-training for theologians in the sciences, and devoting greater attention to the conceptual and methodological questions relevant for dialogue.[34]

Beyond the lingering logical positivism that Smedes identifies, theological engagement with the sciences has often amounted to the theologian reflecting on the implications of particular scientific theories (with varying levels of comprehension), or 'cherry-picking' scientific insights that support their theological commitments.[35] While there is a place for a unidirectional interpretation of scientific insights into a theological register, there is a stronger need for work that thoughtfully considers how both conversation partners can make a real contribution.[36]

In the years since Smedes' diagnosis, we can see these recommendations taken up (though not directly as a result of Smedes' critique) in various different approaches within science and religion. The discipline has given much attention to self-definition and the articulation and interrogation of distinct methodologies, seen in the specific projects of 'science-engaged theology' and 'after science and religion'.[37] Numerous cross-training initiatives have been funded and deployed, encouraging theologians to learn directly from scientists in subdisciplines relevant to their research.

To explore further the notion of 'science-engaged theology', Perry and Leidenhag discuss the need for theologians wishing to engage the sciences in theological construction to develop a 'trading zone' with relevant scientific fields.[38] In this trading zone, the language may be rudimentary (i.e. pidgin), and directly engaging with fluent speakers of the language native to the relevant science will likely assist understanding more than simply reading published scientific literature.[39] Against the giving of heuristic priority to the sciences that Smedes critiques in science and religion scholarship, Perry and Leidenhag argue that in a science-engaged theology the sciences are treated as

---

[34] Smedes (2008, 25).
[35] Calloway and Strawn (2020).
[36] For an example of the latter, see Davison (2021).
[37] For an account of 'science-engaged theology' see Perry and Leidenhag (2023). The 'After Science and Religion' project is described in Harrison and Milbank (2022); Harrison and Tyson (2022).
[38] Perry and Leidenhag (2023, 66).
[39] Perry and Leidenhag (2023, 66).

a source for theological construction without being made an authority, useful for constructive theology yet requiring attention to the way in which scientific thought is influenced by theological and philosophical assumptions already.[40]

Joshua Reeves has also considered the ways in which theologians may meaningfully interact with the sciences in their work. The particular concern he writes to address is the tendency of theologians to conscript scientific methodology to boost the credibility of their scholarship, a flawed strategy that he argues is built on a mistaken understanding of science. Reeves proposes several ways forward; one model suggests that theologians can serve as 'historians of the present'.[41] This is a descriptive stance, grounded in an anti-essentialist approach to science, that brings the strengths of humanities scholarship to the analysis of contemporary scientific understanding and knowledge production. Theologians operating in this mode relinquish normative claims in favour of 'build[ing] bridges of understanding between different communities'.[42] This thread will be picked up later in this section in thinking through how science fiction in particular might function in a mediating role.

## 2.2 The Imagination in Science and Religion

Histories and analyses of the science and religion field give us insights into how its origins and leading thinkers have shaped the methodologies and priorities of recent scholarship. Several recent assessments of the field have already been mentioned (Smedes, Reeves), and the detailed accounts they provide offer helpful background to the arguments of the present work. In previous research I have traced the particular impact of these historical factors for how the imagination is conceptualised in much of the field.[43] In summary, I suggested that the prevalence of particular of scientific methodologies at the beginnings of science and religion scholarship has resulted in the attenuation of research focusing on the importance on the human imagination from a science and religion perspective. The last decade has seen corrective endeavours; however, the field still has a way to go to catch up with the larger turn towards the imagination that we can identify in theological scholarship and in particular scientific disciplines more discretely.[44]

There are good theological foundations upon which we might argue for the importance of the imagination. This work is premised on the notion that

---

[40] Perry and Leidenhag (2023, 2–4).
[41] Reeves (2019, 122).
[42] Reeves (2019, 130).
[43] Lorrimar (2022a, chapter 4).
[44] Lorrimar (2022a, 155).

human creativity is a divine gift, and derived from divine creativity.[45] We communicate using symbols and metaphors (to be discussed further in the next section on embodiment). As inherently imaginative creatures, who make sense of the world and our experiences through story, this aspect of our nature ought to be taken into account in how we approach our task as theologians.

### 2.3 The Contribution of Science Fiction

In yet another assessment of the science and religion field and its future direction, Michael Burdett affirms that the imagination has been neglected within the science and religion field and calls for a more sustained dialogue with the humanities. He singles out science fiction (which he identifies as "the cradle of the scientific imagination") as a critical resource for understanding what people believe about subjects relevant to science and religion.[46] The remainder of this section will therefore turn to the ways in which science fiction might be a part of science and religion scholarship in light of the methodological context explored earlier.

We might start off by acknowledging the value of reading (and writing) fiction in and of itself. As mentioned earlier, the imagination is a fundamental part of our created being. By reading or writing fiction, we are exercising our God-given creative capacity. We often understand things better through image and story, in ways that are formative. Theologian James K. A. Smith writes about the role of the imagination in moral formation, and describes how 'stories seep into us – and stay there and haunt us – more than a report on the facts'.[47] Stories appeal to our imagination and affect, which operate at a precognitive level.[48]

Fiction can convey the messiness of human existence, illustrating the advantages and disadvantages of certain beliefs, worldviews, behaviours, technologies, social structures, and so on without offering propositional evaluations or distilling complex moral reasoning into an ethical checklist. The substantial body of work on theology and literature attests to the significance of literature in understanding ourselves and the world we live in. This is additionally backed up by recent emphases in evolutionary and cognitive sciences that explore the centrality of narrative in human reasoning.[49]

---

[45] For a more comprehensive argument, see Lorrimar (2022b); Lorrimar (2022a).

[46] Burdett (2017, 760). This has since been demonstrated in a recent volume which engages several works of science fiction among other literary texts in relation to science and religion (Fuller (2022)).

[47] J. K. A. Smith (2009, 58).

[48] J. K. A. Smith (2009, 53).

[49] I discuss some of the relevant scholarship at greater length in Lorrimar (2022a, 188–193). The journal *Evolutionary Studies in Imaginative Culture* is also a helpful resource for understanding the role of story in human evolution and thought.

These are some of the ways in which fiction (generally) can assist theological reflection (generally), all of which are also applicable to the narrower context of science fiction in relation to topics at the intersection of theology and science. Building on Reeves' proposal for scholars of science and religion to act as 'historians of the present', I have suggested previously that we might expand the types of scholarship that perform this descriptionist task to include creative media as well.[50] Engaging this response, Reeves acknowledges that 'science and religion scholars, who have been trained to move easily between scientific and religious frames of reference, are ones who can offer imaginative renderings of the larger world picture'.[51]

Though Reeves focuses on science and religion scholarship in his proposal, mediating between positions that occupy different epistemic territories is precisely what *fiction* does really well. Fiction also has the capacity to probe assumptions (e.g. the metaphysical commitments that underpin certain technologies, even when technologists claim a more objective position) and invite reflection without being prescriptive. And it can often do so in a far more disarming fashion than the more propositional mode of academic scholarship.

How can fiction as a medium facilitate the bridge-building between science and religion recommended by Reeves? Fictional characters can be far more direct, even hyperbolic, in expressing a position, and are often able to do so without raising the hackles of readers who ascribe to competing viewpoints. The ideas we find in fiction may conform to or repudiate particular understandings in the real world, but they are a step removed and we do not usually interpret them as making truth claims. In this way, fictional treatments of real world questions and conflicts may perform a mediating role in more philosophical discourse.

The value of science fiction as a mediator between science and theology lies in part in its location outside both disciplines. Rather than having to insert theological questions or claims into scientific research, or translate scientific insights into a theological context, science fiction is a separate meeting ground entirely. The idea that science fiction might serve as an interdisciplinary mediator is not a new one – it has even been heralded as the bridge between the 'two cultures' of science and the humanities.[52] At the same time, the perception of science fiction as a less sophisticated niche within genre fiction parallels the persisting sense that the humanities are inferior to the sciences within the academy.[53]

---

[50] Lorrimar (2020).
[51] Reeves (2020, 835).
[52] Westfahl and Slusser (2009); c.f. Snow (1961).
[53] Imfeld (2021, 123).

If we are able to move away from the negative associations of science fiction, some of the genre's characteristics could be re-framed in terms of strengths common to the sciences and the humanities. For example, Farah Mendlesohn purports that 'in a genre predicated on the thought experiment, theological discourse comes naturally' – the curiosity and capacity for exploring new possibilities in the sciences and the humanities can come together in science fiction.[54]

But we must take care with how we read science fiction in this context. Zoë Lehmann Imfeld challenges the idea of science fiction as a mediator, rejecting the pressing of the genre into service for science communication in a way that subordinates the literary nature of the text.[55] As a literary scholar, Imfeld wrestles with how to undertake interdisciplinary work while maintaining the integrity of the literature she studies *as literature*. She proposes, in agreement with Seo-Young Chu, that science fiction must be understood as the 'violent yoking' of science and fiction, and in resisting actions that might soothe the violence of the yoking (e.g. focusing on the utility of the genre for scientific discourse) we leave room for the 'fruitfully disruptive potential of literature'.[56] In recognising this violent yoking without attempting to diminish it, Imfeld contends that the literary perspective in the interdisciplinary approach of the 'literature and science' field illuminates by subverting hasty transitions and translations between discourses.[57]

While I *am* describing science fiction as a potential mediator between theology and science, I do not wish to prematurely resolve any tensions between the two perspectives. Ideas – both scientific and theological – change when they are translated into fiction, so it is important to engage science fiction as *literature*, just as Imfeld recommends, rather than as prescriptive texts. It must be emphasised that fiction is generally not the place to go for nuanced theological exposition. In part, I have opted not to use explicitly Christian science fiction texts throughout this work because it can be tempting to read too much into the details of the narrative. Authors use allegories; for example, Tolkien's 'Ainulindalë' story might give us some ideas of how he understands human creativity in relation to divine creativity, but we can hardly read it as his definitive theology of creation. Rather, fiction might furnish us with images that help to solidify our theological understanding (or prompt us to question it!).

When it comes to the particular topics featured in the second part of this work, it makes even more sense to draw on science fiction. The genre is so prominent in the 'non-fiction' writings of futurists, it provides an ideal entry

---

[54] Mendlesohn (2003, 274–275).
[55] Imfeld (2021, 123).
[56] Imfeld (2021, 131), c.f. Chu (2010).
[57] Imfeld (2021, 131).

point for theological interlocutors to join the conversation. *Wired* author Michael Solana attends to how influential science fiction has been in cultural perceptions of technology, and implores contemporary writers in the genre to make the most of that influence:

> Our dystopian obsession has grown up in our nightmares as a true monster, which can only be countered by something truly beautiful. Simply, we need a hero. Our fears are demons in our fiction placing our utopia at risk, but we must not run from them. We must stand up and defeat them. Artificial intelligence, longevity therapy, biotechnology, nuclear energy – it is in our power to create a brilliant world, but we must tell ourselves a story where our tools empower us to do it. To every young writer out there obsessed with genre, consider our slowly coalescing counterculture, and wonder what side of this you're standing on.... The time is fit for us to dream again.[58]

The following sections consider how science fiction helps us dream about particular technological futures, and how it might also guide our theological imagination in response to such imaginings. While science fiction can undoubtedly transport topics that have theological import into discussions among scientists, or between scientists and theologians, the particular focus in this work will be how science fiction can mediate between scientific discovery and theological reflection for theologians. The bridging role that science fiction performs here is an expositional one; fleshing out potential societal implications of various technological proposals in ways that prompt theologians to consider how they might also inform theological construction (or adjudication between theological perspectives).

This brings me to a final prologomenal note concerning the relationship between science and technology. The 'science' aspect of the science and religion field has mostly tended to denote the natural sciences; an analysis or critique of this narrower construal of science is beyond the scope of the current work. We are seeing a broadening in what counts as 'science' in the field (aided by the work of Harrison, Reeves, and others in dismantling essentialist understandings of science), evidenced in the embracing of the human and social sciences as disciplines for theological engagement. My own science and religion scholarship is informed by the field of Science and Technology Studies (STS perspectives were an important element of my formal training in a science and religion doctoral programme), and thus affirms the notion of 'technoscience' – which 'signals a deep commitment to the view that [science and technology] are inextricably intertwined'.[59] I will thus draw on both scientific findings and technological scenarios and applications, recognising

---

[58] Solana (14 August 2014).
[59] Jasanoff (2017, 177).

that technology neither serves as a simple proxy for science or constitutes 'applied science' but instead scientific discovery and technological innovation exist in mutual relationship.[60]

## 3 Embodiment

> Here I am, awake and alive – whoever I am. *I'm Robin, aren't I?* I have a slew of fuzzy memories, traces left behind by memory washes that blur my earlier lives into an impressionist haze. I had to look up my own age shortly after I woke. Turns out I'm nearly seven billion seconds old, though I have the emotional stability of a postadolescent a tenth that age. Once upon a time people who lived even two gigaseconds were senescent. How can I be so old yet feel so young and inexperienced?
> 
> …. The letter from my earlier self said I was an academic, a military historian specializing in religious manias, sleeper cults, and emergent dark ages. If so, I don't remember any of it at all. Maybe it's buried deep, to re-emerge when I need it – and maybe it's gone for good. Whatever grade of memory excision my earlier self requested must have been perilously close to a total wipe.[61]

Thus Stross describes the experience of Robin, who has lived far longer than any human lifetime so far by leaving behind his physical body for a virtual existence (Stross' imagined world will be explored further later in this section). Bodies are the ongoing site of philosophical and theological contention for any number of reasons. For centuries, philosophers have wrestled over the relationship between the mind and the body, and over the nature of consciousness in relation to physical matter. Contemporary debates and inequalities involving gender, sexuality, race, and disability are all related to bodily differences. We are increasingly aware of how intergenerational trauma is inscribed in our bodies.[62] Political battle lines have been drawn over bodily autonomy when it comes to reproductive and end-of-life choices.

Embodiment is also a central issue when it comes to human augmentation technologies. These technologies hold out the promise of 'enhanced' physical capacities, and greater morphological freedom for the purposes of optimisation, aesthetics, or both. Technological augmentation is often associated with 'transhumanism', commonly understood to be a philosophical movement that intentionally deploys technological tools to improve human capacities in some way (physical, intellectual, emotional, spiritual, etc.).[63]

---

[60] Jasanoff (2017).
[61] Stross (2006, ch.1).
[62] van der Kolk (2014).
[63] In reality, transhumanism is an umbrella term encompassing diverse movements and philosophies ranging from the punk Grinder communities to the more elite technofuturisms of most of the figures discussed in this section. For one analysis of this diversity, see Boss (2022).

While many technological augmentations modify bodies in physiological ways, technologists and science fiction authors are increasingly imagining an existence *without* a body, inhabiting virtual platforms with endless lifetimes no longer bound by the finitude or frailty of the biological body.

## 3.1 Mind-Uploading

A prime example of a proposed technological augmentation that might discard the body altogether is mind-uploading, an envisioned future technological scenario in which the human brain can be scanned, copied, and uploaded in its entirety onto a computer substrate. It was popularised by roboticist and technofuturist Hans Moravec in his 1988 work *Mind Children*. The ability to upload our minds promises not only immortality (in digital form) and security (our memories can be 'backed up'), but also cognitive enhancement via the use of more efficient "compilers".

Moravec's fellow technofuturist Nick Bostrom, founder of the World Transhumanist Association, has written several wildly optimistic letters from a hypothetical future uploaded self, promising joy and capability beyond our present, limited imaginations. 'What I feel is as far beyond feelings as what I think is beyond thoughts,' writes this hypothetical future self, urging us in the present towards a 'reconfigured physical situation through technology'.[64]

Mind-uploading proposals are often underscored by a contempt for the physical bodies we currently exist in. Moravec, for example, dismisses the physical body, separated from its information systems, as 'mere jelly'.[65] Mark Dery summarises the attitude of mind-uploading advocates to the flesh:

> It's the body's job to be a symbol of detestable putridity in the eyes of an information society characterized by an exaltation of mind and a contempt for matter, most of all the body – that aging, earth-bound relic of Darwinian evolution that Net junkies refer to as meat.[66]

We find this same language of 'meat bodies' in the cyperpunk genre – for example, Case, the protagonist in William Gibson's *Neuromancer* (1984) uses the term to describe his own body in unaugmented form, cut off from cyberspace. The *Bladerunner* franchise is perhaps the most familiar example of cyberpunk fiction, and scholars of the genre argue that cyberpunk culture is so pervasive it has now become our 'quotidian reality',[67] with cyberpunk 'a fictional attempt to grapple with the realities of our postmodern condition'.[68]

---

[64] Bostrom (2008, 2–3).
[65] Moravec (1988, 117).
[66] Dery (1999, 142).
[67] McFarlane, Schmeink, and Murphy (2019, 3).
[68] Booker and Thomas (2009, 110).

## 3.2 Artificial Intelligence

The discourse around mind-uploading often overlaps with that surrounding the increasing sophistication of artificial intelligence (AI) technologies. Artificial intelligence was defined as a specific field in the 1950s, operating under the premise that 'every aspect of learning or any other feature of intelligence can in principle be so precisely described that a machine can be made to simulate it.'[69] Proponents of AI believe that human intelligence is reducible to formal logic and a set of symbols (an idea that shows up in the thought of both Ludwig Wittgenstein and Thomas Hobbes), thus can be translated into equivalent computer processes.[70] Distinctions are typically made between narrow and general AI, with the former excelling at specific tasks within a limited domain, and the latter involving capacities more akin to human cognition. For the purposes of this section, the implications of general AI and even 'superintelligent' beings are most relevant.

Robert Geraci brings together both AI and mind-uploading in his description of 'apocalyptic AI', which imagines that 'in the very near future technological progress will allow us to build supremely intelligent machines and to copy our own minds into machines so that we can live forever in a virtual realm of cyberspace.'[71]

In many respects, however, artificial intelligence research runs counter to the goal of mind-uploading. A growing number of AI researchers are instead centring embodiment in their work; indeed, AI is one of the scholarly strands in the broader embodied cognition field. Matej Hoffman and Rolf Pfeifer, for example, demonstrate that embodied AI is better able to process information, due to its capacity to interact with the environment through movement and sensors.[72] The fact that many AI companionship services price voice interactions at more premium levels than simpler chatbot conversations suggests that more substantial embodiment makes a difference to how we perceive and interact with AI.[73]

## 3.3 The Singularity

Mind-uploading proposals and artificial intelligence also come together in the notion of the Singularity. In fact, the term 'Singularity' was first used in science

---

[69] Moor (2006).
[70] Herzfeld (2023, 5); c.f. Hobbes (1958, 45); Wittgenstein (1960, 1.1, 2.01).
[71] Geraci (2010, 8).
[72] Hoffman and Pfeifer (2012).
[73] For a first-hand account of this experience, see Anna Oakes and Diego Senior, hosts, 'Looking for a Friend', Bot Love (podcast), 15 February 2023, www.radiotopia.fm/podcasts/bot-love.

fiction by futurist Vernon Vinge to describe a future progression of human intelligence beyond our capacity to extrapolate from or model on present intelligence.[74] The idea of the Singularity has been taken up within the field of artificial intelligence to describe the exponential growth of artificial intelligence, and the uncertainty associated with a future in which the intelligence of artificial agents outstrips that of humans by orders of magnitude.[75] It metaphorically deploys an astrophysical concept – a Singularity denotes the breakdown of space-time laws at the centre of a black hole – to highlight the radical shift in existence it represents.[76] The related term "event horizon" (the surface of a black hole, at which point the gravitational pull becomes irresistible) has also been translated into the AI context to convey the inevitability of a Singularity once the tipping point is reached.[77] Technofuturist Ray Kurzweil further popularised the term, describing the Singularity as 'a future period during which the pace of technological change will be so rapid, its impact so deep, that human life will be irreversibly transformed' (and predicted this will occur in the year 2045).[78]

Part prediction, part prophesy, the Singularity attracts a range of responses. As a hypothetical future, it has fuelled a range of research initiatives (e.g. Eliezer Yudkowski's Singularity Institute for Artificial Intelligence) and philanthropic endeavours (mainly via the effective altruism movement, and its longtermism philosophy offspring).[79] Since the large-scale roll-out of accessible generative AI applications in 2022, the effective altruism and long-termism communities have been divided over appropriate responses and the management of AI existential risk.[80]

Beth Singler explores the use of religion in AI-Singularity science fiction texts, particularly as they deal with the 'event horizon' that Vinge's Singularity represents for imagining the human future.[81] She describes religion as a 'pernicious problem' for narratives exploring humanity's response to existential AI concerns.[82] While depictions of religion in post-Singularity tales vary widely, Singler draws our attention to the way in which Doctorow and Stross are able to represent both traditional religious fundamentalism and Singularitarian fervour as similar systems of belief in their novel *The Rapture of the Nerds* (2012).[83]

---

[74] Vinge (1986, 108–111).
[75] Thorstad (2024).
[76] Goode (2019).
[77] Goode (2019).
[78] Kurzweil (2005, 7).
[79] Thorstad (2024).
[80] Wilhelm (2023).
[81] Singler (2022, 138).
[82] Singler (2022, 139).
[83] Singler (2022, 140).

## 3.4 Engaging Science Fiction on Embodiment

Event horizon difficulties notwithstanding, mind-uploading is a fertile scenario for science fiction. Quoted at the beginning of this section, Charles Stross' novel *Glasshouse* (2006) portrays a post-Singularity world, populated only by those who chose to upload their minds prior to the transformative event. Contra to the utopian picture painted by Bostrom et al., Stross imagines a society overrun with identity theft and censorship, and cut adrift from the past due to the expunging of memory by malevolent viruses. On the whole, people still tend to adopt some form of a physical body, which can be modified beyond the still popular "orthohuman" configuration and changed frequently. These bodies are vulnerable to damage and decay, but they are also easily replaceable. This morphological freedom comes with a much greater freedom of expression and identity for individuals (represented as an improvement over our present experience).

The enduring presence and significance of bodies in Stross' imaginary future provides an alternative vision of mind-uploading in which jettisoning the physical body is not necessary. In entertaining this possible future – an activity that speculative fiction invites us into – theologians and philosophers deeply committed to the value of the body and its critical place in human being might contemplate the myriad other implications of mind-uploading for how we exist as individuals and in society.

Even as Stross extends and challenges imagined future ideals relating to mind-uploading proposals, he offers a critique of contemporary social realities. The plot centres around an experiment in which volunteers are recruited to take part in an immersive re-creation of twentieth-century society. Stross describes his intention: 'why not take the Stanford Prison Study protocol and apply it to gender roles among a bunch of posthumans …[in a world] in which physiology and gender and biology are mutable?'[84] Would people conform to the hierarchical and discriminatory social practices of an earlier era?[85]

In Stross' imagined future, people are now described as 'emotional machines' – virtual minds that originated from human brains. AI entities operate alongside these emotional machines, for example, as therapists, or as non-player characters in the immersion. The experiment around which the plot revolves is intended to reconstruct the social relationships from the 'early emotion-age culture' (i.e. our own contemporary and recent social context),

---

[84] Charles Stross, 'Cribsheet: Glasshouse', Charlie's Diary, 13 June 2013, www.antipope.org/charlie/blog-static/2013/06/crib-sheet-glasshouse.html.

[85] Note that Stross wrote this before the questioning of the Stanford Prison Study results as part of the contemporary replication crisis in experimental psychology.

which have been lost as a result of incompatible data formats and military censorship. From this post-Singularity perspective, our own time is described as a polity in which 'people have no control over who they are' with a 'pre-Acceleration scarcity economy'.[86]

Stross brings to life the risks of mind uploading. Our hearts race as the main character tries to evade unknown, but dangerous, enemies. 'If they've hacked my backup so deeply that they can force a new body plan on me, then they can do anything they want. Mess with my head, run multiple copies of me, access my private keys, even make a zombie body and use it to do whatever they want it to do while masquerading as me.'[87] Certainly the story has more impact than a theoretical risk assessment of a speculative technology.

The narrative also allows us to come at certain insights or perspectives from a less confronting angle. Within the experiment, one of the participants is critiquing the study design, suggesting it has oversimplified in its stark gender divisions. 'If I had to guess, I'd say they've mistaken radical prescriptive documentation for descriptive,' she concludes.[88] We are invited to reflect on the cultural and social constraints that are historical from our own vantage point, but which seem limited or based on flawed understanding, and encouraged into greater epistemic humility over our present convictions. Along with all of the risks and disadvantages associated with mind uploading that Stross draws our attention to, the opportunities it might provide for individual expression and play are illustrated as well. The novel teases out the complexities of these technological proposals, neither embracing them nor rejecting them outright, making it an excellent meeting ground upon which we might have the broader theological and philosophical debates (as described in the previous section).

How do we even begin to think theologically about AI and mind-uploading? These technologies have wide-ranging implications for theology, from our understanding of what it means to be human (including human agency, and the extent to which we are genuinely creative), to the expectations that Christians hold for salvation, redemption, and glorification.

Beginning at the end, visions of the future that feature mind-uploading and intelligent machines often have strong eschatological connotations. Geraci underscores the religious connection, arguing that:

> Apocalyptic AI is a technological faith that directly borrows its sacred worldview from apocalyptic Judaism and Christianity. Like these, it refers to (1) a dualistic view of the world, which is (2) aggravated by a sense of alienation

---

[86] Stross (2006, ch.2).
[87] Stross (2006, ch.3).
[88] Stross (2006, ch.4).

that can be resolved only through (3) the establishment of a radically transcendent new world that abolishes the dualism and requires (4) radically purified bodies for its inhabitants. The apocalyptic worldview has deeply penetrated the technological worldview of modern life.[89]

There are particular resonances between AI and mind-uploading and the more gnostic elements of traditional religions (the 'dualistic' worldview that Geraci mentions in the quote earlier). Gnosticism sees the material world (including the body) as evil, a shackle for the spirit which is good and pure. The 'radically purified bodies' that Geraci describes as required for the transcendent future imagined by proponents of apocalyptic AI represent a shift away from the organic, degenerating corporeality we presently endure, albeit in the direction of software existence rather than the non-corporeal spirits of more conventional gnosticism.[90] The tenor of these imaginings is brought to life in science fiction examples such as the short story by Richard Stallman 'Made for you' (2012). The story aims at a utopia, in which a human gradually migrates his existence onto a virtual platform throughout the progression of his relationship with a virtual 'soul mate'. Once the upload is complete, he experiences a more comprehensive joy than he ever could have imagined in his flesh-bound existence. It is a less compelling picture of fulfilling relationship than the one Stross fills out for us (the event-horizon of the Singularity appears to be less of an impediment for Stross' imagination than most), but nevertheless gives us a more tangible understanding of what mind-uploading represents for many (it aligns with Bostrom's euphoric predictions, for example) for our theological and ethical reflection.

Geraci goes as far as to name transhumanism as a new religious movement, that 'advances technoscientific research agendas, creates the ideology for virtual life, and presses for the acceptance of intelligent machines into human culture'.[91] Certain works of science fiction aid in making the ideological implications and/or potential consequences of these technological proposals explicit. For example, Neal Stephenson's *Fall; or, Dodge in Hell* (2019) features billionaire Dodge, whose cryogenically preserved brain is scanned and uploaded by one of his descendants. In Stephenson's tale, uploaded minds inhabit a digital afterlife that most resembles a mediaeval fantasy world (reminiscent of

---

[89] Geraci (2010, 36–37).

[90] David Kelsey is more scathing about the parallels, writing that 'the cultural irony is that a hard-nosed, "godless and anti-humanist"cutting-edge physical science yields an anthropology that is a near cousin to hyper-spiritual second-century gnostic anthropological dualism' (Kelsey, 2002, 8).

[91] Geraci (2010, 6). Brent Waters makes a similar conclusion, describing transhumanism (he uses the term 'posthumanism') as a 'contending postmodern religion' (Waters, 2006, 79).

C.S. Lewis' *Narnia*). Religion features quite overtly, with one uploaded mind self-styling as a deity and making a run for world domination.

Pseudoreligions may have their own scriptures, and in some cases science fiction may fill this role. Joshua Raulerson describes a speculative 'hyperreal' feedback loop that is ever tightening within some techno-utopian and fringe science movements that advocate for

> a vision of Singularity that increasingly recognizes little if any meaningful distinction whatsoever between its fictive and nonfictive representations, reading both SF and futurist nonfiction as scripts for a redemptive future they await with the oracular self-assurance of the devout.[92]

Former evangelical Christian Meghan O'Gieblyn lends weight to the understanding of transhumanism as a religious substitute, recounting her own disillusionment with Christian faith and discovery of transhumanist philosophy as a satisfying alternative.

> Transhumanism offered a vision of redemption without the thorny problems of divine justice. It was an evolutionary approach to eschatology, one in which humanity took it upon itself to bring about the final glorification of the body and could not be blamed if the path to redemption was messy or inefficient.[93]

Just how similar is this glorified body of the transhumanist imagination that O'Gieblyn refers to compared with a Christian understanding of glorification? Well that depends on which perspective you encounter within the Christian tradition, as gnosticism has influenced Christian thought in various ways throughout its history. N.T. Wright is one of those who calls out the pervasive influence of gnosticism, which has led some to a 'souls in transit' notion of the future, whereby Christians hope to leave behind fallen material existence altogether for eternity in spirit form.[94] This version of immortality is a great deal closer to the hopes of many transhumanists than the alternative Wright defends as true to the scriptures and their testimony concerning the body.

Despite the ongoing influence and appeal of gnosticism, bodies matter immensely within Christian orthodoxy. Formulated against various heterodoxies and heresies that included gnosticism, the Apostles' creed affirms a belief in 'the resurrection of the body' and Christians have expressed this hope in liturgy for centuries. But how is this generally understood? Two opposing views

---

[92] Raulerson (2013, 5).
[93] O'Gieblyn (18 April 2017).
[94] Wright (2004). Wright also decries the other extreme, in which Christian visions of the future take their cues from a trenchant 'progress myth', which considers history marching inevitably towards a liberal democratic utopia through evolution, science, technology, and enlightened thought as the natural outcome of evolutionary optimism.

on the bodily resurrection are represented well in *The Meaning of Jesus* (1999) by Wright and another New Testament scholar, Marcus Borg. The latter follows a demythologising tradition, arguing that it is not necessary for Christ to have physically risen from the dead for Easter to carry religious meaning, and even truth.[95] Wright defends the traditional Christian doctrine of bodily resurrection against more metaphorical understandings.

> The personal hope for resurrection is located within the larger hope for the renewal of all creation, for God's new heavens and new earth. Take away the bodily resurrection, however, and what are you left with? The development of private spirituality, leading to a disembodied life after death: the denial of the goodness of creation, your own body included. If Jesus' resurrection involved the abandoning of his body, it would make exactly the wrong metaphorical point.[96]

While there are continuing debates on how precisely the bodily resurrection is understood among Christian theologians which will not be explored for reasons of scope, for Noreen Herzfeld the doctrine underscores the crucial difference between Christian eschatological hope and technofuturist or transhumanist alternative futures. The cybernetic immortality of mind-uploading represents a 'quasi-Cartesian dualism' counter to the resurrection of the body insisted upon in Christian theology.[97] By conceiving of the person in informational terms, 'the dreams of cybernetic immortality fail to capture the full nature of what it means to be human and are illusory hopes for a form of immortality not requiring the action of a supernatural being'.[98] Michael Burdett and King-Ho Leung analyse the informational ontology that operates within transhumanism, revealing how the infosphere takes on a pseudosupernatural nature in proposals such as mind-uploading.[99] Comparatively speaking, the glorified bodies anticipated in Christian eschatology represent a more audacious hope than mere software immortality.

But the body is not merely significant from an eschatological perspective. A theology that affirms the material body in the goodness of creation is well positioned to consider *why* the body matters, what we might lose if bodies are entirely jettisoned. Here, the related fields of metaphor studies and embodied cognition offer crucial insights concerning how our understanding and communication are dependent on our shared bodily experiences. In their seminal text *Metaphors We Live By* (1980), George Lakoff and Mark Johnson explicate

---

[95] Wright and Borg (1999, 131,137).
[96] Wright and Borg (1999, 127).
[97] Herzfeld (2016, 85).
[98] Herzfeld (2016, 84).
[99] Burdett and Leung (2023).

the fundamental embodiment of the metaphors we use everyday. For example, when we talk of a 'warm welcome', we are actually referring to the universal bodily experience that associates physical affection with an increase in temperature. According to Lakoff and Johnson, 'our metaphors will reflect our commonplace experiences in the world. Inevitably, many primary metaphors are universal because everybody has basically the same kinds of bodies and brains and lives in basically the same kinds of environments.'[100] These embodied concepts form the basis for more abstract ones via metaphorical projection.[101] Iain McGilchrist emphases this bodily foundation, arguing that 'everything has to be expressed in terms of something else, and those something elses eventually have to come back to the body'.[102]

Embodied cognition is an interdisciplinary field that brings together research programmes as diverse as philosophy of mind, psychology, neuroimaging, linguistics, robotics, and artificial intelligence. It challenges more traditional approaches to cognitive science that have tended to isolate the cognitive processes of the mind from the sensory context of the body. This includes computational models of the mind, that sees the brain as a self-contained processor that receives sensory input alone from the rest of the body.[103]

Embodied cognition instead underscores the idea that the mind does not operate solely within the brain as a central processing unit. Cognition involves the whole body. Andy Clark summarises this integrated understanding of cognition, emphatically asserting that human brains 'are not the brains of disembodied spirits conveniently glued into ambulant, corporeal shells of flesh and blood'.[104] This perspective is critical for engaging with proposals such as mind-uploading, artificial intelligence, and the Singularity, which predominantly operate in conjunction with the older computational models of the human mind.[105] We see these competing visions of the mind play out in fictional works too, such as Robert Sawyer's *Mindscan* (2005).[106] Sawyer imagines a rather bleak mind-uploading scenario which results in an identity crisis as biological and digital selves clash over which is more authentic.

All this means that it is not only our practices, but also our conceptualising, intellectualising, and therefore our theologising that are embodied.[107] Tobias Tanton offers a comprehensive theological treatment of embodied cognition to

---

[100] Lakoff and Johnson (1980/2003, 257).
[101] Lakoff and Johnson (1980/2003, 497).
[102] McGilchrist (2009, 16), 116.
[103] Gigerenzer and Goldstein (1996).
[104] Clark (1997, 215).
[105] Chalmers (2010).
[106] Sawyer (2005).
[107] Lorrimar (2019, 203).

contend that our theological reflection is inescapably corporeal.[108] Theology is not merely a cerebral collection of concepts, doctrines and beliefs – these facets are all grounded in bodily experience and, conversely, bodily practices in the form of religious rituals also shape theological concepts.[109]

Tanton begins with a problem: 'Theology, then, readily operates under the illusion that it is being undertaken by disembodied creatures who have access to "pure" reasoning, rather than the idiosyncratic mind afforded by a bundle of flesh and bone, neuron and sinew, the products of a long evolutionary process.'[110] Against this problem, he makes the case that the notion of embodied cognition provides the necessary context for how we understand revelation, accommodated as it is to the human mind. Our corporeality determines the constraints within which our understanding can operate, and therefore the context in which divine revelation must be mediated.[111] Studying human cognition gives us greater insight into revelation (how it is mediated, not its content), according to Tanton.[112]

Embodied cognition offers insights not only for how God communicates with us, and how we understand God, but for how we communicate with and understand disembodied intelligent beings such as hypothetical uploaded minds or AI. We have a tendency to anthropomorphise AI when we talk about it, attributing to it belief, knowledge and understanding. At the same time, we can also underestimate how involved humans are in current AI applications. At present, even disembodied AI technologies depend on embodied information. Large Language Models, for example, which operate in most of the generative AI models used presently (e.g. ChatGPT) are trained by humans on data produced by humans, and therefore rely secondhand on language derived from physical corporeality.[113] Stross highlights this fact in the context of mind-uploading – one of the characters in the immersive embodied simulation observes 'it is very interesting to discover that the phrase "my blood runs cold" actually reflects a physical sensation'.[114] Through this fictional perspective of an uploaded mind experiencing the full sensory landscape of a human body, we are made cognisant of how communication and understanding depend on our bodies.

What does this mean for the prospect of AI? Can it truly attain to the capacities of human cognition? Andrew Davison draws on the theological tradition

---

[108] Tanton (2023).
[109] Tanton (2023, 3).
[110] Tanton (2023, 7).
[111] Tanton (2023, 15–16).
[112] Tanton (2023, 23).
[113] Lorrimar (2023).
[114] Stross (2006, ch.15).

of analogy to describe how artificial intelligence resembles human cognition without being identical to it.[115] As Davison highlights, this is an example of how philosophical thought can inform our understanding more broadly – in this case by way of analogy we might choose certain words and concepts to describe AI capacities while maintaining a distinction to how the same words and concepts are used of human capacities. Davison leaves open the question of what this might mean for the future achievements of machine learning, however, especially concerning the authenticity of 'understanding' in the context of metaphorical language that originates in human embodiment.

We can imagine in theory (if not in concrete detail, given the limitations of our corporeality), that new metaphors might arise which transcend physicality, and do not depend on a shared bodily experience for effective communication.[116] Tanton's use of accommodation to explain how an infinite God can be intelligible at all to the shape of the human mind might have further applications here as a framework for conceiving of understanding across seemingly unbridgeable ontological divides. This is admittedly conjecture, but could accommodation also occur between embodied human and virtual or AI minds, or even between the latter and God?

In a similarly speculative vein, theological responses to AI are also concerned with the implications for how we understand human being, and whether the category of human could ever extend to AI. Herzfeld gives an excellent overview of the history and development of AI technologies, arguing that some definitions and approaches understand human intelligence to be primarily rational, while others construe it in terms of relationality.[117] Much scholarship in theological anthropology focuses on the Christian claim that humans are created in the image of God, and Herzfeld also takes up this doctrine in thinking about the technological creations of our own making.

The *imago Dei* has often been pressed into theological service to underscore human uniqueness (considered further in the next section), and to define what it means to be human. Interpretations of precisely what the *imago Dei* corresponds to are generally characterised as substantive (a characteristic that humans possess), functional (a role that humans perform), or relational (the *imago Dei* comprises the fundamental relationality of humans – to God, to

---

[115] Davison (2021).
[116] We might also consider the implications of the fact that many humans already experience the world in particular bodily configurations that also limit a direct embodied experience of particular metaphors. A person who experiences total paralysis, or complete sensory deprivation, for example, will not 'know' that physical proximity equals warmth in the same way as someone who has that sensory exposure. In many ways we are already looking to overcome different contextual realities in search of a shared language.
[117] Herzfeld (2023, 9–13).

each other, etc.). Historically, a substantive account that associates the *imago Dei* with the capacity for reason has been dominant, but this has given way in more recent years to functional or relational interpretations.[118]

It is worth noting that the doctrine of the image of God has been highly contested throughout the history of its interpretation, and there are only a few Scriptural references upon which interpretations are built.[119] Particular framings of the *imago Dei* have wrought significant harm, justifying social hierarchies and the exclusion of many deemed to lack the necessary defining characteristics.[120] We must not rely too heavily on the doctrine for a theological anthropology, however, heeding Jeanine Thweatt-Bates' reminder: 'Despite its importance and centrality, the biblical concept of the *imago Dei* remains ambiguous, prompting a long history of theological interpretation of this primary and yet stubbornly mysterious aspect of human being.'[121]

Alongside the *imago Dei*, many theological engagements with AI have centred on the matter of personhood; that is, is it possible for a robot or other AI entity to be a person? In answering this question, Herzfeld employs Martin Buber's I-Thou distinction (via Barth's developed criteria) – we relate to persons as 'thou' but to objects as 'it'. She ultimately concludes that we cannot exist in I-Thou relationship with AI, but must instead maintain an understanding that they are tools, not people.[122] As with the *imago Dei*, personhood is also notoriously difficult to define as a concept, particularly in such a way that it does not unwittingly exclude some humans from the category of person. The question of how cyberspace and virtual technologies are reconfiguring our relationships is a subject of contemporary theological interest, pushing the boundaries of how we define human being.[123]

Returning to science fiction, *Klara and the Sun* (2021) by Kazuo Ishiguro raises this very question of personhood in relation to artificial intelligence. It is difficult to avoid spoilers, but the plot centres on whether an "artificial friend" (i.e. an android) can be a satisfying replacement for a human loved one. The artificial friend Klara is astounding for being both utterly different (e.g. her perception of the sun, the way she processes visual sensory inputs, her perspective on what makes for a fulfilling life) and remarkably "human" (e.g. her compassion, her longing to be chosen). The tale delivers a subtle but incisive challenge as we contrast Klara's seemingly naive worldview with our own

---

[118] Cortez (2010, 30).
[119] Kelsey (2009, 896).
[120] Voss Roberts (2017, xix).
[121] Thweatt-Bates (2012, 109).
[122] Herzfeld (2023, 174–175).
[123] Midson and O'Donnell (2020).

assumptions about what makes us *us*, and whether than can be defined using scientific frameworks.

Of course, just because we imagine AI to share many characteristically human attributes does not mean it is true. Humans have a propensity to anthropomorphise. Science fiction does give insight into how we perceive AI though, and when it comes to personhood, science fiction can be revelatory in relation to many of our hopes for AI. We often attribute 'human' identities to AI beings in fiction. Apart from Klara in Ishiguro's novel, we might look to the work of Becky Chambers (discussed in the next section), or Martha Well's *The Murderbot Diaries* for AI protagonists that exhibit human-like capacities for introspection, compassion, emotional intelligence, and growth. The way we respond to AIs in fiction suggests that we at least *hope* that they might come to share in personhood, and extend our options for meaningful relationships.

Indeed, we find this hope reflected in real-world applications also. People *are* turning to AI to meet their individual relational needs. Responses to these trends are conflicted – some decry the developments as yet another symptom of the widespread malaise initiated and exacerbated by the rise of social media; others welcome the expansion of social networks for the otherwise lonely and neglected in society. The science fiction examples offered in this section invite us into imaginaries that are hospitable to theological revisions when it comes to personhood, such as Midson's rejection of a Buberian I-Thou framework. As an alternative, Midson suggests we might 'emphasize plurality by figuring "*We*" alongside "Thou" to convey how we – humans and chatbots alike – are congeries of different relational parts – including other humans and chatbots'.[124]

### 3.4.1 Which Bodies?

Most of these shifting understandings of personhood, and how we interpret the *imago Dei* still see the body as essential to human being. Even as we accord continued significance to embodiment against extreme proposals for mind uploading and disembodied artificial intelligence, we are left with challenges. In attempts to augment or extend human capabilities through technology, what exactly ought we preserve? Who decides this? In a critique of Western humanisms, post-colonial novelist and philosopher Sylvia Wynter traces the emergence of the 'ethnoclass Man', a male, Euro-centric religious form of the human that exists in antagonistic relation to various subhuman 'others'.[125]

---

[124] Midson and O'Donnell (2020), 159.
[125] Wynter (2003). For a related deconstruction of humanism, see the discussion of critical posthumanism beginning on page 37.

A very particular conception of human being has been developed and reified (especially in enhancement discourse), and we therefore need to critically examine how such ideals have come to be encoded in our technologies.[126]

The technofuturist visions described earlier in this section comprise one iteration of transhumanism. There are many other forms which are constructed on divergent commitments regarding the nature and purpose of human being. Jacob Boss highlights vastly different types of transhumanism in his contrasting of 'punk' and 'profiteering' approaches to human technological augmentation.[127] Whereas more elite forms of transhumanism take the form of what Boss terms 'corporate medical futurism', punk transhumanism generally operates extra-institutionally and is more aligned with genuine justice.[128] Rejecting the push for immortality, punk transhumanism turns emphatically towards the body and aesthetics, and therefore eschews the gnosticism of transhumanisms that promote mind-uploading and radical longevity. Philip Butler engages transhumanism from the perspective of black liberation theology, expressing his goal to 'imagine what it means to begin utilizing technology's personally augmenting capabilities to enhance human spiritual experiences'.[129] This version of transhumanism promotes the melding of technology and spirituality as crucial for black liberation from oppression, and offers a perspective on technological augmentation that could powerfully inform broader transhumanist thought.

Again, we may look to science fiction as a medium for reflecting on these alternative transhumanisms – these challenges to the elitist technofutures that have taken up so much space in academic and cultural discourse find more fertile ground in the speculative genre. Afrofuturism, for example, is a movement that blends science fiction with African diaspora culture. It represents 'a way of imagining possible futures through a black cultural lens'.[130] Octavia Butler's *Dawn* is a prime example of an Afrofuturist science fiction novel. According to Justin Mann's analysis, the protagonist Lilith subverts hierarchical forces (racism, misogyny, nationalism) and 'recasts human survival in terms of adaptation and evolution rather than conservation and maintenance'.[131] Technology is very present in Butler's imagined future, but human augmentation is carried out according to motives and objectives vastly different to the more elite transhumanist visions of what Boss terms 'corporate medical futurism'.[132]

---

[126] Midson (2018, 193).
[127] Boss (2022, 135–139).
[128] Boss (2022, 136).
[129] P. Butler (2020, 1).
[130] Womack (2013, 9).
[131] Mann (2018, 62).
[132] Boss (2022, 136).

The Chinese genre of immortality cultivation fiction represents a non-white instantiation of transhumanism that 'strives to rebel against rather than replicate' colonial depictions of the ideal human.[133] In contrast to most Western visions of technological immortality, the enhancement project described in these Chinese works of immortality cultivation 'builds a public cultivation/education system open to all, promotes cooperation rather than competition, and writes into its constitution the social obligations of accomplished cultivators to care for the less powerful and disenfranchised.'[134]

More broadly, postcolonial studies shows how non-Western approaches have often been better able to resist dichotomising reason and imagination, mind and body, and so on in ways that are really productive in the current conversations in theological anthropology. Kwok Pui-lan, for example, points out that one of the goals of postcolonial studies is to 'unmask colonial epistemological frameworks [and] unravel Eurocentric logic.'[135] These are the very contexts that produced the more elitist transhumanist philosophies, so surely they require greater scrutiny.

While theological perspectives encourage us to value the body, and to listen to a diverse array of perspectives when it comes to how bodies are configured, we must also take care not to uncritically celebrate the physical over the virtual. Although the fact that many of our interactions (professional and social) occur online today has increased isolation in some circumstances, it has also overcome it in others. Theologians, philosophers, and cultural critics have been preoccupied with the danger of substituting relationships with AI in the place of meaningful human interactions. But is this the only way to think about AI? Might it be possible to have meaningful interactions and relationships with artificially intelligent entities while acknowledging they are different from human-human relationships? Does ruling out an "I-Thou" characterisation to such relationships strip them of their value altogether?

Of course, the increasing use of robots as companions for the elderly should challenge us to examine our priorities, but there are other instances in which AI might facilitate important dimensions of our lives. Though machine learning is very much in its infancy, early studies are showing it could be effective for administrating cognitive behavioural therapy (CBT) for conditions such as chronic pain.[136] When more of the shortcomings of present generative AI

---

[133] Ni (2020); c.f. Ali (2019).
[134] Ni (2020, 764).
[135] Kwok (2005, 2).
[136] Piette et al. (2022). While this does not negate the importance of human therapists, there are nevertheless specific therapeutic modes and situations that could be well managed using AI technologies, and this drastically increases access.

technologies are overcome, we can imagine a future in which people (especially children) have their own personal tutor, one whom they relate to with warmth and even perhaps friendship. And certainly Ishiguro's *Klara and the Sun* challenges us to think about how AI might provide companionship in ways that supplement, rather than replace, human relationships.

In checking some of the technofuturistic enthusiasm for radical proposals such as mind-uploading, therefore, it is important that we do not retreat into an extreme conservatism over what is normative for human bodies or relationships. The limitations of the doctrine of the *imago Dei* were alluded to earlier, but one inference that we may reasonably infer concerns the malleability of human nature. As Kathryn Tanner concludes so helpfully:

> Human beings must not only be changeable but susceptible to radical transformation beyond the limits of their own – or any – created nature. Human beings through divine power become what they are not and have no capacity of being by themselves: human versions of the divine image itself. They therefore must have a created nature that does put rigid bounds on what they can become. They must not be limited by their own nature in the way other things are, but must have the capacity in some strong sense to become other things.[137]

Tanner is operating from the premise that the original creation had a *telos*, a dynamic purpose, rather than a static perfection. Here she draws on patristic thinkers like Irenaeus, or Gregory of Nyssa. Although it is fair to say that the type of growth they were describing is more in the realm of spiritual or moral growth, and anything like contemporary biotechnological enhancement would not have entered into their imagination, their understanding of creation with a *telos* is more compatible with the idea that technology can shape human becoming than the notion of return to a primeval perfection.

On the flip side of these growth eschatologies is a version of Christian hope that looks back to Eden, looking to recapture that original state of perfection. Often negative responses to technology set it up in opposition to pure or unspoiled nature. An oversimplistic rationale is at work: if something is natural then it must be good, if it is artificial, then it is bad. Bronislaw Szerzsinski describes the emergence of this binary:

> From the late eighteenth century nature started to be seen in various ways as the unspoilt, as an Edenic arena of goodness and innocence, unsullied by the artifice, alienation and corruption of modern life … nature came to take on new sacral meanings, as a counterpoint to the increased technologisation of society.[138]

---

[137] Tanner (2009, 40).
[138] Szerszynski (2005, 102).

This underlying nostalgia for Edenic innocence is particularly troubling if we apply it to the human condition, telling as it does a story of human identity (i.e. original innocence) that does not map very well onto the insights we gain from evolutionary science, strips us of agency in our own formation, and risks drawing harmful boundaries around what is normative for human nature.

If we take embodiment seriously, but also eschew a theological anthropology that prescribes a narrow physiological definition of what comprises a normative human body, then we inhabit a space in which both openness and discernment are required. Language evolves, and there is the possibility that metaphors might emerge from disembodied AI or uploaded minds that do not refer to a shared bodily experience in the same way our present metaphors do. This represents a challenge, but also potentially an opportunity, for the theological task of seeking new understanding and new ways to express timeless truths in each new era.[139] A good starting point is to acknowledge that the anticipation of radical bodily transformation was a feature of religious apocalypticism long before transhumanism existed as a worldview.[140]

While some versions of the futures envisioned by transhumanists do warrant critique (e.g. a radical mind-uploading approach that does away with bodies entirely), the idea of using enhancement technologies to alter human being and living is not inherently wrong, and does not always run counter to a theological understanding of what it means to be human, or to a Christian hope in what we are becoming. If we understand that human being is malleable, and that technology is a fundamental element of the creativity gifted us by our creator God, and we understand the perfection of creation in teleological terms, then technological enhancement might instead be framed as something that requires the graces of wisdom and discernment, rather than outright prohibition.[141]

And finally, we are not only technological but imaginative creatures, and this recommends a particular mode of dialogue with these future possibilities. We have seen already how works of science fiction can assist theological reflection when it comes to the ongoing significance of bodies, and how we think about normativity; it can be a way into both critique and construction. *Glasshouse* is a prime example – while some events and characters represent a more gnostic disdain for the body (for example, the disgust displayed by participants of the simulation as they encounter the physiological realities of menstruation), the novel also pushes us to interrogate how historical biases have shaped our definitions of 'normal' and the boundaries we draw around human being.

---

[139] Lorrimar (2019, 203).
[140] Lorrimar (2019, 200).
[141] For a more comprehensive treatment of these claims, see Lorrimar (2022a).

Cyberpunk was mentioned earlier in this section as a genre characterised by a contempt for the physical body that is also evident in strands of transhumanism. Julia Grillmayr writes that

> cyberpunk shows bodies and minds that are constantly altered, enhanced, or perverted by bio- and nanotechnological prostheses, cognitive implants, and/or new orifices that interface with digital networks and cyberspatial domains. The definition of what it means to be human becomes slippery in cyberpunk as categories of identity, nature, and essence crumble.[142]

Grillmayr draws on cyberpunk fiction to tease out the very different perspectives of transhumanism and critical posthumanism, which are often unfortunately conflated. A broader survey of fiction addressing technological futures reveals that there are ways to imagine the evolution of minds and bodies that do not elevate the former at the expense of the latter. Singler describes some recent works of science fiction (including Stross' post-Singularity futures) as 'post-cyberpunk', 'marked by an emphasis on embodiment and its attendant place in a society that requires social justice, an ethos that is counter to the dislike and fear of our "meat bodies" often noted in earlier cyberspace paeons'.[143] The contribution of critical posthumanism to how we think about human being will be explored in the next section. The fifth section will develop this further in relation to disability, a topic that again invites us to think about the nature of human being in relation to our corporeality.

## 4 Human Uniqueness

### 4.1 Human and Non-Human Nature

'I have placed you at the very center of the world.'[144] So speaks God to man (and undoubtedly it was a *man* imagined as the recipient of such a proclamation), according to fifteenth-century humanist Giovanni Pico della Mirandola. The question of how humans are distinct from non-human nature is a perennial one, with particular attributes highlighted as singular to human being (e.g. reason, possession of a soul, imagination, religiosity). Human uniqueness is often the basis of arguments for human exceptionalism, and the attribution of moral status to human beings over other species.

The notion of human uniqueness has a complicated legacy within Christian theology and its influence on Western philosophy and culture more broadly.[145]

---

[142] Grillmayr (2019, 273).
[143] Singler (2022, 139).
[144] Pico della Mirandola (1956, 7).
[145] Some content in this section has been adapted from material published in Lorrimar (2025, forthcoming).

Together with the assertion that humans are created in God's image (Gen 1:26-28), God's subsequent directive to Adam and Eve to 'fill and subdue' the earth (Gen 1:28) has informed countless theological anthropologies that emphasise human dominion over nature. Perhaps nothing exemplifies this dominion so much as the description of the human task as the enslavement of nature given by Francis Bacon, often styled the 'father of modern science', who extended earlier humanist visions of dominion by uniting them with the grandiose aspirations of modern empirical science.[146]

Lynn White Jnr's famous 1967 critique of Western Christianity finds the root of the contemporary ecological crisis in the triumph of Christian anthropocentrism over paganism in the mediaeval period.[147] According to White, the Christian doctrine of humans made in the image of God established a dualism between humans and the rest of creation, and instrumentalised nature in relation to human ends.[148] White describes how this doctrinally driven anthropocentrism was embedded into the foundations of modern science and technology as it developed in the West.

The question of human uniqueness is also relevant to the themes of earlier sections. Anthropocentrism is rife in contemporary movements that advocate for the use of technologies to 'enhance' human characteristics. Transhumanist advocates of enhancement acknowledge the continuities between their position and earlier humanisms from the Renaissance and Enlightenment periods.[149] The perceived special status of humans is threatened by the advent of artificial intelligence. Much of our social, not to mention theological, engagements with the ethical questions around AI are consumed with the question of whether AI might be accorded personhood. Furthermore, the differential status we see applied between humans and non-humans has its parallels in the various distinctions and discriminations often made between humans according to race, class, gender, able-bodiedness, and more.

## 4.2 Engaging Science Fiction on Human Uniqueness

In her award-winning *Wayfarer* series, Becky Chambers writes what has been termed 'hope punk', a style of science fiction that presents a more positive vision of the future than is typical for the genre. Chambers imagines a universe

---

[146] Bacon (1964, 62.).
[147] White Jr (1967).
[148] White Jr (1967, 1205). Anthropocentrism manifests most clearly in understandings of the human task that emphasise dominion over the creation, but it is also present to a lesser degree in stewardship models too. For more detail on the insufficiency of the *imago Dei* construct as a foundation for theological anthropology, see Lorrimar (2025, forthcoming).
[149] Bostrom (2005, 1–4); Bostrom (2003, 39–40).

in which humans are not at the top of the intelligence pyramid, and there are many other highly intelligent sentient species outside of our solar system. In this imagined universe, humans have had to learn humility, and they are far from morally (or intellectually) superior to the other species that make up the fictional Galactic Commons. They possess little power and influence politically – Jeremy Axelrod suggests that humans occupy the condition of subalternality in Chambers' fictional world.[150]

Chambers' oevre might have been deployed in relation to any of the themes treated in the current text. With respect to embodiment, Chambers offers a critique of anthropocentric enhancement projects. In the second book of the *Wayfarer* series, *A Closed and Common Orbit* (2016), we gradually learn of the 'Enhanced Humanity' movement, which operates Enhancement Colonies in which genetically engineered humans are bred in gestation chambers for specific purposes (reminiscent of Aldous Huxley's famous *Brave New World*). The Galactic Commons and the human diaspora have severed all ties with the movement, thus indicating universal condemnation of their project.[151]

The flourishing societies depicted in Chambers' fiction are thoroughly embodied and sensual. Bodily differences are celebrated and delighted in via physical encounters between species, sometimes platonic, sometimes sexual. A lot of attention is given to culinary descriptions, with hospitality at the table an important feature of most communities and societies throughout Chambers' works. The relationship between the body and its environment is treated with spiritual reverence, with detailed funeral rites and composting of corpses described in the third *Wayfarer* novel *Record of a Spaceborn Few* (2019).

Chambers also gives us a picture of what the human task might look like in a world no longer ruled by anthropocentrism. This concern is particularly central to her *Monk and Robot* novella series. Set on the fictional moon Panga, they depict a world in which, at some time in the distant past, robots had awakened to consciousness, discovered and rejected their created purpose, and departed for life on their own in the wilderness (a far cry from the Singularity envisioned by many technologists and sci-fi authors). Not only were the humans of Panga able to relinquish control and reach peaceful accord with the robots, but in the intervening years they have found a way to live more lightly. Much of the cultivated territory is given back over to wilderness, and human societies operate sustainably and justly. The main character, Dex, is a tea monk – equal parts priest, therapist, and tea sommelier, Dex travels the regions brewing up bespoke herbal blends for troubled souls and providing space for contemplation.

---

[150] Axelrod (2018, 319); c.f. Spivak and Morris (2010).
[151] An analysis of Chamber's engagement with transhumanism in *A Closed and Common Orbit* can be found in Roldán Romero (2022).

For various reasons, Dex finds themself in the wilderness, beyond the reaches of human territories. They encounter Mosscap, a robot who has come as an emissary to the humans to understand a driving question: 'what do humans need?'. The remainder of the novellas see them journeying together in search of answers to this question, and learning of one another's customs and worldview along the way. While facilitating an uncomfortable interaction between Mosscap and a community that has rejected technology, Dex reflects on how their ministry has prepared them, musing that 'building a canvas for others to explore themselves on was rather the point of monastic service, after all'.[152]

This celebration of difference goes hand in hand with other societal reorientations. Throughout the novellas, Dex is reflecting on the relationship between identity, vocation, and purpose. Pangan society has shifted away from an economics of capital, to one that acknowledges mutual benefit in a wider exchange of goods and services. Chambers would be the first to acknowledge the many influences on her writing and we see similar themes in classic works of science fiction. Octavia Butler's *Xenogenesis* series also critiques the hierarchical nature of human society and psychology, while maintaining a place for genetic engineering technologies in the construction of a better world. Butler's *Earthseed* series proffers a new religious movement to address socioeconomical and political crises, and also imagines a life for humans in the universe beyond Earth. Ursula Le Guin's *The Dispossessed* (1974) falls within the critical utopian tradition (in which we might also situate Chambers' work), imagining an anarchist-syndicalist alternative to capitalism.[153] An earlier novel in the same series, *The Left Hand of Darkness* (1969), develops an alternative construal of sex and gender and examines the cultural implications. While Le Guin herself recognised and lamented a lingering assumption of heterosexuality in the text,[154] her writings helped pioneer a tradition of questioning norms.

Of course, Chambers and the authors that inspire her portray fictional universes populated with other clearly sentient species. It remains a hypothetical scenario for us, but that does not mean there are not lessons to be drawn from the human self-understanding that she depicts. How do we balance an acknowledgement of particularly human capacities that come with attendant responsibility, without inflating our worth compared with other creatures? Elizabeth Johnson articulates the concern well:

> We have advanced capabilities to respond to other beings, to imagine the thought worlds of others, to act out of a sense of moral obligation, to respond

---

[152] Chambers (2022).
[153] For an excellent analysis of the social structure in *The Dispossessed*, see Stainforth and Walton (2019).
[154] Le Guin (1989).

aesthetically to the beauty of nature, even to praise the Creator of that beauty. Despite our unique capacities for language, reason, morality, and love, however, the human legacy is becoming the erasure of others on the tree of life.[155]

Johnson's diagnosis is reminiscent of White Jnr's critique. Though White was pessimistic about the potential for science and technology, grounded as they are in Christian attitudes asserting the mastery of humans over nature, to solve 'disastrous ecologic backlash', he was not entirely despairing over how theology might shape our view of nature into the future.[156] He identifies the Franciscan emphasis on the equality and autonomy of all creatures as a remedy, arguing that a problem of religious origin necessitates a religious solution.[157]

### 4.2.1 Deep incarnation

Johnson prescribes a similar remedy to White, situating humans firmly in the community of creation and grounding her theological anthropology in a deep incarnation model.[158] Deep incarnation understands Christ's incarnation in solidarity with *all* flesh (i.e. all biological existence), rather than limiting its representation to humanity.[159] The incarnation is framed cosmically, and in evolutionary perspective, reckoning with the pain, violence, death and contingency inherent in nature and presenting a God who is ultimately and intimately concerned with the suffering and healing of all creation.[160] This cosmic Christology draws support from scriptural texts such as Colossians 1:15 (Christ is the 'firstborn of *all* creation', emphasis added), and lends itself to an ecological emphasis apparent in recent theological trajectories emphasising the mutuality of human dignity, social justice and creation dignity. The 2015 papal encyclical *Laudato Si'* offers a prime example, tying ecological concerns together with God's special solidarity with the poor, and stressing the kenotic aspect of incarnation in this context.[161]

Consistent with a deep incarnational frame, David Clough focuses his theological reflections on nonhuman animals, as both subjects in their own right but also necessary to a robust theological anthropology.[162] He distinguishes between various types of anthropocentrism: 'perspectival anthropocentrism'

---

[155] E. Johnson (2014, 214).
[156] White Jr (1967, 1206).
[157] White Jr (1967, 1207).
[158] E. Johnson (2014).
[159] Gregerson (2001).
[160] Sollereder (2019); Southgate (2008).
[161] Francis (2015).
[162] Clough (2013).

acknowledges that as humans we are primarily concerned with the way in which God relates to humans, 'epistemological anthropocentrism' attests that we only have access to theological knowledge related to God's dealings with humans, and 'teleological anthropocentrism' makes the claim that the world is created by God for the sake of humans.[163] While the first two types are legitimate accommodations to our contextuality, Clough refutes the view that the entirety of nonhuman nature exists as a backdrop to the special relationship that God enjoys only with humans. Such a position is based on an impoverished understanding of the purpose of creation, which extends beyond redemption to the participation of *all* creation in the triune life of God.[164]

### 4.2.2 Critical Posthumanism

Going beyond explicitly theological materials, the field of critical posthumanism might also resource theological responses to anthropocentrism. Critical posthumanism is concerned with a deconstruction of humanism and its assumptions (especially human exceptionalism), and a rewriting of humanity against this complex legacy.[165] Rejecting the dualism inherent in traditional humanisms, posthumanism situates the human in a relational ontology. In rethinking what it means to be human in non-anthropocentric terms, critical posthumanism can inform how we use and conceive of technology and how we relate to non-human creatures.[166]

The figure most strongly associated with posthumanism is Donna Haraway, who proposed the 'cyborg' figure as a reimagining of how humans relate to non-human beings.[167] The cyborg is an organism-machine hybrid, and is intended to trouble various binaries that characterise humanist thought (nature/culture, male/female, self/other, human/animal). The cyborg prefigures Haraway's later work on companion species, which frames the human in symbiotic relations with micro- and macro-organisms.[168]

Posthumanism is concerned with not only the relationship between human and nonhuman entities, but also the overcoming of historical and present social distinctions (the various binaries mentioned earlier being interdependent in a

---

[163] Clough (2013, xviii).
[164] Clough (2013, 6).
[165] Herbrechter (2018).
[166] Critical posthumanism ought not be confused with transhumanism, a philosophical movement that advocates for the technological enhancement of human capacities.
[167] Haraway (1991). It should be noted from the outset that Haraway's proposal is woefully insufficient when it comes to the topic of disability. This is discussed further in the next section.
[168] Haraway (2008). Indeed, both the cyborg and the companion species are brought alongside one another as complementary concepts in the more recent volume *Manifestly Haraway* (Minneapolis, MN: University of Minnesota Press, 2016).

dualistic approach to the world, if one is troubled then so are others). Similar to Wynter's critique of the 'ethnoclass Man',[169] Haraway's call to reimagine the human centres around the question '*Cui bono?*' Who benefits, who is considered human and participates in the posthuman future?[170] In the posthuman context, the 'others' excluded from the modern humanist subject 're-emerge with a vengeance'.[171]

Other prominent posthumanist thinkers include Rosi Braidotti and N. Katherine Hayles. Braidotti surveys a range of positions that comprise what she considers to be the posthuman condition, identifying a shift towards seeing nature and culture in continuity as the common characteristic.[172] In line with this continuity, Hayles emphasises the way in which technology has always been bound up in human identity – we are inextricable from the material and informational networks in which we are embedded.[173] For Hayles, 'the posthuman evokes the exhilarating prospect of getting out of some of the old boxes and opening up new ways of thinking about what being human means'.[174]

The posthuman turn to a nature–culture continuum thus simultaneously reconfigures our relationship to animals and to technology.[175] Nonhuman others (i.e. the environment, animals, machines, even God) are no longer defined only in terms of their relationship to us. There is a mutuality that Haraway captures in the notion of 'becoming with', and at the same time she highlights the context of our microbial makeup in a way that reveals the idea of a unique 'human' category to be a nonsensical one.[176] With their focus on relationships across species (including AI), fluid representations of gender and sexuality, ecological sensitivity, and transformed political and economic structures, we might reasonably describe Chambers' fictional worlds as a depiction of posthuman becoming. Human exceptionalism is relegated to the past, spoken of as a warning against hubris and attributed to the destruction of earth and the crumbling of human 'civilisation'.

While Chambers' works celebrate embodiment, this does not lead to a rejection of artificial intelligence. Her critique of human exceptionalism also extends to how we generally think about artificial intelligence. We meet Lovelace in Chamber's first work, *The Long Way to a Small, Angry Planet* (2015), an AI who controls the computer systems aboard the *Wayfarer* spaceship. From the

---

[169] See page 27.
[170] As cited in Star (1991, 43).
[171] Braidotti (2013, 37).
[172] Braidotti (2013, 2).
[173] Hayles (2012).
[174] Hayles (1999, 285).
[175] Wolfe (2010, xvi).
[176] Haraway (2008, 4).

beginning Lovelace is depicted as a person, with a mind that works in ways completely distinct from human intelligence. In a conversation on the subject of human assumptions, Lovelace expresses her frustration.

> They act like all AIs want a body. Granted, I think *I* do, but that doesn't mean all of us do. That's such an incredibly organic bias, the idea that your squishy physical existence is some sort of pinnacle that all programs aspire to.[177]

In the sequel, *A Closed and Common Orbit,* the story centres on Lovelace as she *does* take on a synthetic humanoid body, and changes her name to Sidra. Having previously experienced the world as a systems AI, she finds the sensory limitations of a single body confining. Here Chambers' imaginings achieve a similar result to Ed Yong's non-fictional work exploring the intricacies of non-human perception – revealing how humans experience the world in a particular, narrow fashion that in no way exhausts the rich sensory landscape of nature.[178] While the Galactic Commons does not extend the same rights to AIs as it does to organic sentient species, Chambers' portrayal of Sidra's identity formation and social interactions are clearly intended to challenge this distinction and its implications for the relationship between organic and inorganic beings. Sidra experiences crises of identity and existential angst that are both unique to her makeup and universal for conscious embodied creatures, developing her own agency and determining for herself how she is most comfortable as a body in a world that blends the physical and the virtual.

Another AI character in the same novel suggests to us that a human or organic body is by no means a prerequisite to a meaningful relationship. Like Sidra, Owl is a systems AI by programming, and the only companion to the human child Jane for many years. Owl essentially raises Jane, an escapee from one of the Enhancement Colonies with no prior knowledge of the outside world, guiding her in her escape and preparing her to live as a human among the many species that make up the Galactic Commons.

While critical posthumanism is often critical of religion and theology, insights from the field have nevertheless been refracted through a theological lens by some scholars. Elaine Graham early on recognised the fruitfulness of posthumanist discourse for theological discussions of human creativity in the context of biotechnology.[179] She argues that a posthuman approach to nature placed within the context of creativity as a divine gift both prevents the reduction of nature to 'technonature' (i.e. in resisting binaries, we must not commit the opposing error of conflation) and the counter tendency to

---

[177] Chambers (2015, 57).
[178] E. Yong (2022).
[179] Graham (2004).

construct overly nostalgic 're-enchantment' narratives.[180] Graham adopts Haraway's cyborg figure as a heuristic tool to eschew 'solutions of either denial or mastery in favour of a post/human ethic grounded in complicity with, not mastery over, non-human nature, animals and machines'.[181] Rather than withdrawing from technologies, we are called, theologically speaking, to engage with them thoughtfully and ethically.[182] Within a posthuman frame, AI cannot 'usurp' human rights and responsibilities, because rights and conscious agency are no longer viewed as the exclusive preserve of human beings.[183]

Theologian Jeanine Thweatt-Bates represents Adam and Eve as cyborgs in the garden,[184] drawing on the hybridity of Haraway's construct as a resistance to the category of the natural without stripping nature of all significance altogether (and thus permitting its instrumentalisation).[185] Thweatt-Bates surveys and offers a textured analysis of how Haraway's cyborgology is influenced by religious ideas, particularly when it comes to the figuration of Christ and sacramentality.[186] For Thweatt-Bates, the theological utility of the cyborg resides in its capacity to highlight the materiality, embeddedness and connectivity of humans within a matrix of technology and nature.[187] Provided the 'cyborg' is able to overcome its narrower science fiction representation á la *Terminator*, it is able to convey the ambivalent orientation that is appropriate in relation to technological possibilities.[188] She contends that a commitment to human uniqueness is still present in many theological engagements with the cyborg construct, even as it is reframed to acknowledge ontological continuity between humans and nonhumans and to emphasise human creativity and technological prowess as key human distinctives.[189]

In her theological appraisal of posthumanism, Thweatt-Bates argues that 'theological work remains to be done ... explicitly connecting the cyborg to theological articulations of hybridity, as expressed within the theologies of those living out the material dimensions of cyborg existence'.[190] While recent theological trajectories that recognise the centrality of bodies to human being may appear to be moving us closer to a posthumanist perspective, the

---

[180] Graham (2004, 195).
[181] Graham (2002b, 228).
[182] Graham (2006, 179–180).
[183] Hayles (1999, 289–290).
[184] This directly contradicts Haraway's claim that 'the cyborg would not recognise the garden of Eden; it is not made of mud and cannot dream of returning to dust', as Thweatt-Bates acknowledges (*A Cyborg Manifesto*, 151; Thweatt-Bates (2012, 172)).
[185] Thweatt-Bates (2012, 27–28).
[186] Thweatt-Bates (2012, 33–34).
[187] Thweatt-Bates (2012, 124–125).
[188] Thweatt-Bates (2012, 132–122); c.f. Graham (2002b, 228).
[189] Thweatt-Bates (2012, 125).
[190] Thweatt-Bates (2012, 151).

discussion of the body in the abstract retains a troubling normativity.[191] She points to disability, queer, and postcolonial theologies as discourses that are able to challenge homogenous accounts of embodiment and bodily naturalism, transgressing categorical boundaries in a posthuman sense.[192] Only once the particularity of embodiment is underscored can Thweatt-Bates present Adam and Eve as cyborg figures:

> Embedded within a nexus of strange boundaries of human and nonhuman relationships – human and divine, human and animal, human and human – the cyborg pair in the Garden are what they are because of the construction and contestation of these boundaries. What does it mean to be made a cyborg in the *imago dei?* Simply to have been made a creature who is simultaneously kin and other: to God, to other humans, and to nonhumans.[193]

Ultimately, human uniqueness resides only in these relationships described; it does not confer elevated status with respect to nonhuman creation.[194]

These are precisely the questions explored in Chambers' *Monk and Robot* novella series, and Dex and Mosscap together seek greater understanding of themselves, and the other. As Dex comes to know Mosscap, the robot's question initial question ('what do humans need?') takes on a reciprocity. Their interactions call into question the assumption of human exceptionalism. To give an example, Dex and Mosscap have a protracted dispute over pronoun use (Mosscap goes by 'it'). Dex argues 'I'd say you're more than just an object.' Mosscap is slightly offended, responding, 'I would never call you *just* an animal, Sibling Dex.... We don't have to fall into the same category to be of equal value.'[195]

As mentioned before, a significant portion of theological reflection on AI has been concerned with the question of personhood. Our conferring of equal status on AI is contingent on it becoming like us.[196] Chambers exposes the anthropocentrism inherent in such thinking, the idea that personhood can only exist in beings that closely resemble humans.

Thweatt-Bates points out that posthumanism not only challenges traditional theological anthropologies, it also has implications for our understanding of God. We have tended to portray God in relation to our own human subjectivity – what happens to our theology of God when our ideas about the human subject evolve? Rather, theological understandings of God that emphasise relationality

---

[191] Thweatt-Bates (2012, 150–151). As mentioned in the previous section, critiquing the bodily ideals embedded in technological proposals is essential theological work (Midson (2018, 193)).
[192] Thweatt-Bates (2012, 151–168).
[193] Thweatt-Bates (2012, 172).
[194] Thweatt-Bates (2012, 172).
[195] Chambers (2021b, 83).
[196] For example, Smith attributes a 'lower form' of personhood to robots, and accords them certain legal protections on the basis that they often serve as proxies for humans, rather than on the basis of any intrinsic worth (J. K. Smith (2022), 51).

(both within the trinitarian Godhead, and with creation) are more aligned with a posthumanist understanding of the subject.[197] Thweatt-Bates argues for a rethinking of Christian spiritual practices such as prayer and discernment in the direction of a more collaborative engagement with the divine, rather than an abnegation of our own will and agency.[198]

The hybridity of Haraway's cyborg has thus inspired new directions in theological construction. Anne Kull adopts the cyborg construct to make sense of the incarnation, aligning with Haraway's own interpretation of Christ as a cyborg of 'trickster' figure.[199] "Destabilizing what it means to be human troubles what it means for God to become human," argues Thweatt-Bates, and this represents an opportunity to rethink some of the dualisms inherent in classic Christology.[200]

Scott Midson deploys Haraway's cyborg to advance theological thinking about nature and technology. In similar fashion to White's call for theological solutions to the ecologic crisis brought about by the impacts of Christian theological developments, Midson suggests that theology must be part of a posthuman imagination.[201] Midson adapts Thweatt-Bates' work in a critical examination of how the technologies we use are premised on particular ideals of what it means to be human, warning against a romanticisation of Edenic innocence that only reinscribes the unhelpful nature/technology binary.[202] Thus we see how critical posthumanism might resource our theological thinking about human being today, particularly against the ecological and technological crises. It is vital that our theological anthropologies do not recapitulate the evolutionary dominion narratives of Bacon and his contemporaries, but can reckon with technology without exalting or condemning it.

Christian theologians might also learn from aspects of critical posthumanism when it comes to the blending of fiction and theorising, the use of imagination in fleshing out the implications of particular moral convictions or theological commitments for the future. Haraway turns to fictional accounts that champion the cyborg figure, acknowledging her debt to authors such as Joanna Russ, Samuel R. Delany, James Tiptree Jr. and Octavia Butler whom she describes as 'theorists for cyborgs' (a similar list today would surely include Becky Chambers).[203]

---

[197] Thweatt-Bates (2012, 148).
[198] Thweatt-Bates (2012, 148).
[199] Kull (2001); Haraway (1992, 90).
[200] Thweatt-Bates (2012, 172). Though Kull and Thweatt-Bates do not refer specifically to deep incarnation, their emphasis on hybridity is hospitable to such a framework.
[201] Midson (2018, 24).
[202] Midson (2018, 63).
[203] Haraway (1991, 173).

Haraway not only draws widely on extant science fiction literature in her scholarly writing, she incorporates her own fictional material. 'The Camille Stories' concludes Haraway's 2016 collection of essays, and is a series of what Haraway terms 'speculative fabulation', a 'mode of attention, a theory of history, and a practice of worlding'.[204] The Camille stories are a collaborative fabulation, following five generations descended from 'a child who had no truck with conventional genders or with human exceptionalism'.[205] The stories imagine a different configuration of kin relations as part of healing ruined places and unpicking the legacy of settler colonialism. Haraway weaves in symbiotic relationships with animal species and technological augmentations in a practical vision of her theoretical work. Haraway describes her purpose in writing: 'The Camille Stories are invitations to participate in a kind of genre fiction committed to strengthening ways to propose near futures, possible futures, and implausible but real nows.'[206]

Scott Midson construes technological explorations in science fiction to be a 'way to usefully begin to rethink how we see ourselves in relation to technologies in ways that do not prefigure the (ideal) human through practices of exclusion'.[207] We might extend this beyond science fiction treatments of technology, to the broader social, political, and economic worlds that science fiction writers imagine for us. The hopeful picture Chambers offers us of humans living in mutually enriching relationships with other species, both sentient and non-sentient, organic and inorganic, and developing and using advanced technologies in ways that attend to the finitude of resources, is an inspiring conversation partner for theological reflection on human being and becoming.

## 5 Disability, Economic Inequality, and Access

How might we put together the emphases on embodiment and hybridity in the preceding two sections, to imagine alternative futures that are both shaped by theological commitments and inspiring for ongoing theological construction and ethical life? If Haraway's collaborative Camille Stories invite folks to propose near futures that are both radical and plausible, virtual reality technologies can provide a platform for testing and enacting those futures.

### 5.1 What Is Virtual Reality?

Virtual reality (VR) technologies combine hardware, software, and user movement to immerse a user in an imagined space that feels real; that is, the brain is

---

[204] Haraway (2016b, 213).
[205] Haraway (2016b, 137).
[206] Haraway (2016b, 136).
[207] Midson (2018, 111).

persuaded into thinking it is somewhere else.[208] Virtual realities can be individual, or shared by multiple users – the collective element leads Matthew Cotton to describe VR as a socio-technical system.[209]

We participate in virtual worlds by assuming an avatar – a digitally embodied representative of ourselves. For some, the avatar is an opportunity to adopt an identity vastly different from how they present in the physical world, whereas others reach for a facsimile. Thus VR allows us to simultaneously become disembodied (our physical bodies fade into the background) and 'hyper-able-bodied' through the expansion of our capabilities via avatars.[210]

For many, the idea of collective VR immediately conjures up images of the 'metaverse'. The metaverse remains a somewhat inchoate concept, but is framed as the next evolution of the internet.[211] Generally, the metaverse combines VR applications across entertainment, education and business to generate a single virtual context in which all aspects of personal and professional life can be conducted.

It was actually science fiction that gave us the term 'metaverse'. Neal Stephenson coined it in his 1992 cyberpunk novel *Snow Crash* to describe the virtual world at the centre of his fictional universe, accessed through personal or public terminals connected to a privately owned network. Stephenson is considered a futurist in his own right, writing near-future science fiction that considers the impact of emerging technologies such as solar geoengineering.[212] One of the earliest 'metaverses' developed is the online media platform *Second Life*, which launched in 2003 and peaked at over a million users a decade later. *Second Life* encourages pseudoanonymity, with users able to sculpt their own avatars and identities separate from the real world.[213] Robert Geraci describes *Second Life*, in the eyes of its users, as 'the precursor to the digital paradise of Apocalyptic AI'.[214]

The idea of the metaverse really entered the mainstream in 2021, many people first becoming aware of the concept when social media giant Facebook rebranded as Meta. Some people have even begun investing in virtual property in the metaverse, without seriously reflecting on the implications of

---

[208] Cotton (2021, 4). For the sake of simplicity, I will be referring to virtual worlds in contrast to the 'real' physical world that we inhabit in our bodies. This is not to diminish the nature of virtual worlds and interactions, as the line between real and virtual worlds is getting blurrier (Geraci (2010, 72)).
[209] Cotton (2021, 4).
[210] Jerreat-Poole (2022, 65).
[211] Cheng (2023, 1).
[212] Stephenson (2021).
[213] Boellstorff (2015).
[214] Geraci (2010, 72).

those particular visions of the future for social structures and activities such as governance, education, healthcare, leisure, and relationships.[215]

Virtual reality has been heralded for many potential benefits. Cotton offers a helpful overview, which includes training and education applications, as well as therapeutic uses, for example, in psychological treatment for phobias.[216] Research continues to investigate whether VR can increase empathy through provision of immersive experiences from the perspective of another. Studies have shown positive changes in people's attitudes towards human rights as a result of VR immersion experiences.[217] The jury is still out on whether VR might facilitate empathy towards racial minorities and decrease implicit bias;[218] however, a recent feasibility study found that VR might increase empathy among disability support workers towards their disabled clients.[219]

## 5.2 Virtual Reality and the Body

While VR has been touted for a number of benefits, it is worth considering the implications it has for how we think of human being. VR is essentially a disembodying technology, even if we occupy avatar bodies. How different is it from the radical mind-uploading proposals discussed in Section 3? Like mind-uploading, virtual reality seeks to overcome some of the restrictions of our typical physiology and embodiment (whereas mind-uploading seems to focus more on increasing longevity and cognitive processing capacity, VR often defies bodily constraints such as how fast we can move through space, or the kinds of athletic feats we can accomplish without injury). If VR technology promises an escape from the limitations of a 'normal' body, what does that mean for how we understand disabled bodies?

## 5.3 Engaging Science Fiction on Virtual Reality and Accessibility

The novel *Lock In* (2014), by John Scalzi, imagines a near future in which a significant proportion of the global population has experienced complete and permanent physical paralysis (Haden's syndrome) as a result of an incurable virus. Combining various technologies discussed in Section 3, 'locked in' individuals (Hadens) are able to access a virtual world (also used widely by individuals not affected by the virus) and control personal robotic transport units in the real world through the use of neural network implants. In many

---

[215] Zhou, Leenders, and Cong (2018).
[216] Cotton (2021, 35).
[217] Bujić et al. (2020).
[218] Tassinari et al. (2022).
[219] Wilding et al. (2022).

respects, these technologies allow disabled individuals to participate more fully in human life (the sequel features a sport dominated by Haden players, but with many fans who are not Hadens).

Because the technological solutions for Haden's syndrome are advanced (the novel takes place twenty years after the initial pandemic event), the cultural and political impacts of these interventions are teased out in the novel. There are political debates and legislative proposals around the rolling back of expensive government support for the various accommodations that Hadens currently receive, on the grounds that technology has advanced so far that Haden's syndrome is no longer functionally a disability. This is explored further in the sequel *Head On* (2020), as the privatisation and commercialisation of industries developing assistive technologies or offering support services increasingly sidelines Hadens without sufficient financial means.

*Lock In* also directly addresses the complexity of 'cure' in the context of disability. One of the individuals living with Hadens raises the issue: 'Making people change because you can't deal with who they are isn't how it's supposed to be done …You say "cure." I hear "you're not human enough".'[220] A cure is being developed for Haden's syndrome, but not all those with the condition are interested in being cured. In parallels to certain perceived disabilities in our world, Hadens are described as having their own community and culture. In fact, Scalzi's related novella explicitly compares the tensions within the Haden's community to the real world deaf community – while some who are deaf see deafness as an impairment they would like to overcome (e.g. by using cochlear implant technology), others see it as an identity marker that gives cohesion to a unique deaf culture with its own language.

## 5.4 Complicating Technology and Disability

Indeed, the idea of technology as the solution to disability is pervasive. 'We are inundated with imagery of disabled people overcoming the circumstances of their bodies through technology, which is framed as a kind of technological salvation for bodies and minds.'[221] Thus writes Ashley Shew in recounting her experience of having a leg amputated, describing how almost everyone she encountered immediately and hopefully (and without prompting) raised the topic of prostheses. When it comes to such aids, technology has tended to be simplistically rendered as enabling crippling disability to be overcome in science fiction imaginings.[222]

---

[220] Scalzi (2014a, 99).
[221] Shew (2023, ch4).
[222] Ewart (2019).

It is worth noting that technology can sometimes *produce* disability, rather than mitigate it.[223] Technological aids, from prostheses to VR headsets, cause their own types of pain and exhaustion, but these are often dismissed or downplayed as worthwhile compromises in service of 'able' bodies.[224] The field of disability studies pushes back against the notion that technology ought to restore physical normality, with Tobin Siebers offering the following description:

> Disability studies does not treat disease or disability, hoping to cure or avoid them; it studies the social meanings, symbols, and stigmas attached to disability identity and asks how they relate to enforced systems of exclusion and oppression, attacking the widespread belief that having an able body and mind determines whether one is a quality human being.[225]

How might insights from disability studies shape our thinking about VR? Adan Jerreat-Poole brings a 'crip technoscience' lens to their engagement with VR in science fiction, citing Aimi Hamraie and Kelly Fritsch's definition of the 'politicized practices of non-compliant knowing-making: world-building and world-dismantling practices by and with disabled people and communities that respond to intersectional systems of power, privilege, and oppression by working within and around them'.[226] Virtual realities tend to be built around able-bodiedness as the most desirable user position,[227] reifying the limitations of the physical spaces we already occupy. Ironically, VR 're-centres the physical body' – the in-game avatar is controlled by out-of-game bodily movements.[228] Jerreat-Poole draws heavily on the 'crip futurity' framework developed by Allison Kafer in order to crip the technology of the VR game, a process which they describe as 'repurposing, hacking, and modding futuristic technology in order to explore justice-oriented relationships between the body, technology, and society'.[229] Jerreat-Poole imagines an alternative VR game that does not merely accommodate crip bodies, but celebrates them, and concludes their article by sketching out the technology and gamescape that might constitute such an alternative.[230]

While this section focuses more specifically on virtual reality in relation to disability, there are other science fiction works that explore disability more

---

[223] Schalk (2020, 412).
[224] Jerreat-Poole (2022, 64).
[225] Siebers (2008, 3–4).
[226] Hamraie and Fritsch (2019, 4–5).
[227] Ellcessor (2016, 2). This is also true of technological solutions such as prostheses, designed to return users to a default standing orientation in the world (Shew (2023, ch4)).
[228] Jerreat-Poole (2022, 65).
[229] Jerreat-Poole (2022, 70); c.f. Kafer (2013, 21).
[230] Jerreat-Poole (2022, 74).

generally. The short story collection *Outlaw Bodies* explores from a number of perspectives the ways in which future bodies might be controlled through enhancements and modifications, and some of the implications for gender and sexual identity, and disability.[231] Ato Quayson takes as his focus the various frames that have been applied to disability in Nobel Prize–winning literature, contending that literature helps to 'refract these multivalent attitudes towards disability'.[232] Kathryn Allan challenges the dominant presentation of technology as cure in an edited volume of essays that explore disability in science fiction.[233] Allan highlights the capacity of science fiction to act as an 'early warning system' for the types of futures that can arise out of our current situation, arguing that this positions the genre uniquely to conceive of future possibilities for constructing disability.[234]

The 'early warning system' of science fiction can be amplified by scholarship. Dan Goodley and Katherine Runswick-Cole draw attention to the way in which many 'disabled' people have not been permitted to occupy the position of the 'modern human subject'.[235] Here we might revisit the idea of the cyborg, premised as it is on deconstructing the assumptions about the subject that were central to humanism and modernity. The previous section highlighted Haraway's cyborgology as a fruitful construct for theological reflection, however it is notably deficient when it comes to disability. Jillian Weise offers a crucial corrective from her own experience of disability, critiquing Haraway's 'A Cyborg Manifesto' for its failure to recognise that the cyborg is a real figure already for disabled folks, and not merely a metaphor for a so-called feminist resistance.[236] Listening to such critiques, this concluding section aims to centre disability as a key consideration in theological discussions of technology and embodiment.

Though Haraway's proposal overlooked the fact that those experiencing various disabilities were already depending on technologies in often life-sustaining ways, other scholars have engaged the cyborg more inclusively in relation to disability. Thweatt-Bates' turn to disability theology was mentioned in the previous section, recognised as a theological trajectory that might trouble traditional notions of embodiment in a posthuman direction. Damien Patrick Williams traces the origins of the cyborg in earlier imaginings about space exploration, and the understanding that the unfamiliar conditions of space

---

[231] Selke and al Ayad (2012).
[232] Quayson (2007, 36).
[233] Allan (2013).
[234] Allan (2013, 3).
[235] Goodley and Runswick-Cole (2016, 3).
[236] Weise (2020).

will engender experiences akin to the social construction of disability that exists presently in life on earth (and therefore disabled people might be better equipped to adapt).[237] 'Had we maintained disabled people's stories as a part of the mythology of the cyborg, from the beginning, Western societies might now have a better relationship with concepts of disability and mental health,' argues Williams.[238] In rehabilitating the notion of the cyborg, which has only served to disenfranchise people living with disabilities, Williams draws on intersectionality theory (with parallels to Hamraie and Fritsch's 'crip technoscience') to recognise the particularities of specific disabilities in relation to identity, politics, and technology.

## 5.5 Economic Access

An intersectional lens brings into focus other forms of marginalisation beyond disability. Scalzi also invites us to consider how a world in which we can interact with others separate from our physical body changes our relationships with traditional classifiers such as gender and race. We never learn the gender of the protagonist Chris, who as a Haden from childhood has never experienced the world in a particularly gendered manner.[239] The way that Scalzi is able to do this with subtlety (many readers do not even notice) is particularly effective for later reflection on how embodiment, technology and gender interact.

Scalzi is not the only writer to explore the place of virtual reality technologies and their implications for access and equity. Ernest Cline's 2011 *Ready Player One* was a bestseller (with polarising reviews) in which characters from all kinds of backgrounds and personal circumstances were able to compete in a worldwide game set on a virtual reality simulator called the OASIS. The use of avatars disguises players' real appearance, which is presented as ameliorating discrimination on the basis of gender, youth, and physical disfigurement. For the main character, the OASIS is aptly named, allowing him to escape the discomforts and deprivations of his daily life of near poverty. Cline's 2020 sequel, *Ready Player Two*, is perhaps best employed to highlight the downsides of VR – while the neural interface technology introduced in the novel supposedly has benefits such as increasing empathy, Cline's presentation is less than convincing.

The ambiguity of science fiction is evident here – a particular work can be strong in its representation of some ideas and the imaginary it builds, while

---

[237] Williams (2019).
[238] Williams (2019).
[239] Two separate audiobook versions are available, so readers can choose either a male or a female narrator for the protagonist.

falling short in other ways. Most science fiction explorations of virtual reality and metaphors retain economic stratification in the societies they depict (possibly a result of the near-future setting that they often adopt). Neal Stephenson, John Scalzi, and Ernest Cline all imagine virtual worlds in which the sophistication of an individual's avatar and/or personal spaces within the metaverse is indicative of their wealth and status.

In thinking about the possibilities for VR to engage disability more helpfully, we need to ensure that we are not just swapping one form of exclusion and injustice for another. Even if they are designed in ways that do not privilege able-bodied participants, within the current technological and economic paradigm VR technologies will only be available to those with sufficient wealth. Bringing together virtual reality and disability, a novella by James Tiptree Jr presents a more cautionary tale in which a physically impaired teenage girl is given a 'dream' opportunity to control a beautiful (but literally brainless) body and celebrity status, only to become the puppet of powerful corporate interests.[240]

Here, the role of science fiction in critiquing present social realities is crucial. While this volume is mainly concerned with science fiction as a conversation partner for the dialogue between science and theology, we could make the case that this also applies to religion and economics (setting aside the question for now of whether economics is a science). Exponential technological advancement is increasing the wealth gap between the most privileged societies and the least. Technology transfer programs have formed part of public policy solutions, with varying success. The field of development economics is concerned with the economic mechanisms of technology transfer, but politicians and policymakers are generally operating at some distance from ethicists and technologists.

How might speculative fiction provide a shared reference point for some of these disciplines to collaborate? Sociologist Jens Beckert contends that fiction and economics have more in common than most would assume. Both 'create a reality of their own by making assertions that go beyond the reporting of empirical facts' and tend to take narrative form.[241] Expectations around economic futures are produced out of uncertainty by economic decision-makers. Imaginaries are at work in both, even if suspension of belief operates differently – we suspend our disbelief in imagined economic futures under the assumption that they will approximate economic reality. There are enough epistemological parallels that they might be productive conversation partners.[242]

---

[240] Tiptree (1973/2004).
[241] Beckert (2016, 61).
[242] Beckert (2016, 62).

Let us briefly consider what this process of exploring technology transfer in fiction could look like based on its applicability in science and religion studies. Scalzi's fiction raises the issue of economic disparities in access to VR technology, but the focus remains within a single nation and associated technological environment. To explore technology transfer specifically, we might return to Charles Stross. Stross' *Merchant Prince* series centres around 'The Clan', a group of families who possess a hereditary capacity for travelling between worlds.[243] Bearing striking resemblance to the Mafia in its organisational structure and the degree of control it exerts over its members, The Clan's power base is located in an alternate history, where Christianity did not take hold, the Industrial Revolution did not occur, and the Eastern seaboard of the landmass known as the United States of America in our world is inhabited by numerous small European principalities. The 'Gruinmarkt', their own kingdom, is a typical mediaeval fiefdom in an agrarian economy. The 'world-walkers', able to travel between their world and our world, have become extremely wealthy and powerful aristocrats through a combination of efficient communications and transport in the world of the Gruinmarkt and trafficking drugs in the United States.

Early on in the series, the existence of further alternative worlds is discovered. A third alternate history becomes part of the storyline: an industrialised 'steampunkesque' world in which the North American continent is the stronghold of the exiled British monarchy (at war with France), social customs are roughly Edwardian, and Levellers are agitating for revolution. While this world is industrial, its technology is pre-WWII in sophistication. For various reasons that need not be discussed so as to avoid spoilers, a small progressive element among the Clan seek refuge in this third timeline, where they establish themselves as part of the post-Revolution 'New Commonwealth' and set about a strategic programme of technology transfer to 'catch up' with the United States in that domain.

Wealth disparity is exacerbated by technological advances. What does ethical technology transfer look like? Is it the responsibility of governments? Is it only appropriate in the context of aid, or a legitimate business enterprise? All of these are questions that concern development economists, but responses would surely be enriched by the input of scholars from various humanities' perspectives, as well as technologists.

The discussion around technology transfer in Stross' series illustrates the various motives operating. First, money. They can amass great personal wealth

---

[243] The first book in the series is Stross (2004). This discussion here refers to content from books across the series; specific books will be only cited where direct quotes are used.

by trafficking in intellectual property. Second, lifestyle – if they are to make this their new home then they have been accustomed to the luxuries afforded by more developed technologies. Third, power. They are able to exchange their access to technological information for positions of power in the government, which also gives them security. Loyalty for homeland is also a factor at times. Erasmus, born in Timeline 3, is a key revolutionary agent dreaming of a more equitable society. Clan member Miriam grew up in the United States, but sees technology as salvation from subsistence and serfdom for the masses in the Gruinmarkt. And, finally, war, or the avoidance of war, is a motivating factor. 'World walkers' having been deemed a terrorist threat in our world, technology transfer contributes to an arms race in which only the threat of 'mutually ensured destruction' maintains a fragile peace between timelines.

The series aids reflection on real-world technology transfer by highlighting the differences. The Clan have the benefit of hindsight to inform which technologies they prioritise for transfer and which to avoid altogether. Technology is not value-neutral, and this is made explicit. One of the government agents of the New Commonwealth puts it well: 'If you choose a technology, you are implicitly accepting the political imperatives that provide the context the technology operates within. If you want railroads, you must accept coal and steel industries, compulsory seizure of land for rights-of-way, standard railway time, and central stations.'[244]

In this fictional account, they also recognise the social context in which technology operates to be even more crucial than the technology itself. Thus, they prioritise contraception and domestic technologies and associated family planning measures to achieve female emancipation and optimise their workforce. In writing their Constitution, they make certain tweaks to human rights language from our timeline in order to prevent liberty from encroaching on egality or fraternity (thus foreclosing the emergence of libertarianism). Having witnessed the abuses of centralised surveillance infrastructure, they are able to transfer information and communication technologies while building in the security structures to prevent a national surveillance system.

Of course, there are further differences. Access to technological information in Stross' world is completely controlled. In our world, migration and business both muddy the waters – it is not so simple as one party having all the technology and then dictating how it is transferred to another. Nor should it be – the Clan's approach to social engineering would smack of paternalism if it could be implemented in our world. This just emphasises the importance of postcolonial

---

[244] Stross (2018, ch.6).

voices in this conversation – the complex legacy of imperialism and enduring privilege means that 'wealthy' nations should not be making these decisions on behalf of 'poor' ones.

There are theological resources that support this reimagining of global economics. Kathryn Tanner proposes a theological economics premised on grace that is admirable in many ways,[245] but has come under criticism for not directly engaging with economic scholarship. Economist Rowena Pecchenino contends that Tanner's proposal that the current market economy structure can be maintained and redeemed by a substitution of motives (with love of God and neighbour supplanting possession) is based on faulty assumptions – in fact worldly goods are finite and therefore competitive in a way that divine grace is not.[246]

Albino Barrera is a professor of both theology and economics, and presents a more sophisticated interdisciplinary engagement. Transfer schemes are one of the pillars in his call for economic decision-makers to consider their mutual obligations.[247] He conceives theologically of economic security as a twofold gift that acknowledges human participation in the divine bestowal of gifts but is also realistic about the nature of material goods. He shows a practitioner's awareness of the various economic and development agencies involved in global economic restructuring.[248]

Questions of equality and access are particularly pertinent in relation to the prospect of human technological enhancement, discussed several times already in this Element. Some transhumanists have presented technological enhancement as a solution to the present inequalities and injustices. Julian Savulescu and Ingmar Persson, for example, advocate for moral bioenhancement as a moral imperative, on the grounds that our present capacities are insufficient to address the catastrophes (environmental, economic, etc.) of contemporary life.[249] Others suggest that cognitive enhancement (even restricted to the few privileged elites) will have trickle-down effects in the form of effective global solutions for systemic injustices.[250]

Elaine Graham calls out the lie in such prognostications, predicting that human enhancement technologies are far more likely to increase existing disparities.

---

[245] Tanner (2005).
[246] Pecchenino (2007).
[247] Barrera (2005).
[248] Barrera (2005).
[249] Persson and Savulescu (2012, 9–10).
[250] For an excellent critique of this problematic stance, see Devenot (2023).

> To privileged first-world citizens, the digital and biotechnological developments bring with them an expansion of selfhood beyond the limits imposed by bodies and minds. To those unable to participate, however, it means further exclusion, compounded by the possibility that due to globalisation, the wealth of Western cyborgs rests on the cheap labour of their third-world sweatshop fellows.[251]

As highlighted in the present section, people can be excluded from augmentation technologies for economic reasons, but also on the basis of disability (physical or cognitive). There is a growing body of work reflecting theologically on disability, with Nancy Eiesland's *The Disabled God* (1994) a significant contribution. Building on liberation and feminist readings, Eiesland argued that the central image of God in the broken body of Christ can properly be construed as a disabled God. Eiesland also writes within a social model of disability, which emphasises the need for accessibility and assistive technologies over cures. To shed light on what it means to think of disability as a social problem, Lennard Davis helpfully distinguishes between impairment and disability: '[i]mpairment is the physical fact of lacking an arm or leg. Disability is the social process that turns an impairment into a negative by creating barriers to access.'[252]

Engaging with fictional depictions of the near future such as Scalzi's can encourage our theological reflections on disability towards a social model, rather than an ontological one. The parallels to debates around identity and cure with respect to deafness were mentioned earlier; there are similar discussions with respect to conditions such as Down's syndrome or autism spectrum disorder (ASD). Sara Green and Donileen Loseke provide a helpful account of the tensions between social and medical narratives of disability and some of the ways this tension impacts disabled people, their family, and their caregivers.[253] The fact that various disability communities are not homogenous when it comes to how they conceive of disability is a reminder of the need to listen intently to those with personal experience (the slogan 'nothing about us without us' has been taken up by many people with disabilities to insist upon this inclusion).

Brian Brock approaches the topic of disability through what he terms a 'theological hermeneutic of experience', sharing an account of life with his son Adam who he describes as profoundly cognitively disabled.[254] Brock

---

[251] Graham (2002a, 69–70).
[252] Davis (2006, 12).
[253] Green and Loseke (2020).
[254] Brock (2019). Brock also acknowledges the difficulty in speaking for his son, who cannot communicate or advocate clearly for himself.

argues that the wounded body of Christ is God's attack on our contemporary assumptions regarding disability, revealing the fundamental error of determining some to be 'able-bodied' in comparison to others.[255]

The crucified Christ is only part of the Christian narrative, however. Atonement theory is beyond the present scope, but the event of the cross is tied to the resurrection in Christian theology. For those who do hold to a physical resurrection (as discussed in Section 3), an understanding of disability is pertinent when it comes to such eschatological expectations. There are a range of theological perspectives when it comes to the topic of impairment and disability in relation to the anticipated resurrection body.

A theology of bodily resurrection goes hand in hand with the affirmation of matter and bodies as good (contra Gnosticism). The main imagery that guides Christian understanding about the nature of the resurrection body comes from 1 Corinthians 15:35-55, a long passage in which the apostle Paul is attempting to describe the eschatological hope in answer to the question: 'How are the dead raised? With what kind of body do they come?' His response somewhat cryptic:

> What is sown is perishable, what is raised is imperishable. It is sown in dishonor, it is raised in glory. It is sown in weakness, it is raised in power. It is sown a physical body, it is raised a spiritual body. If there is a physical body, there is also a spiritual body. (1 Cor 15:42)

What do we take the description of the resurrected body – imperishable, glorious, powerful, spiritual – to mean? Does it include the eradication of all disabilities? It did for the majority of early Christian theologians, argues biblical scholar Candida Moss, who outlines how thinkers such as Irenaeus and Augustine linked salvation and the cleansing of sin with the removal of all bodily deformities or impairments through the healing work of Christ.[256]

With the rise of disability theology, however, this is no longer an unchallenged belief. Though the scriptures on the nature of the resurrected body are difficult to interpret, particularly in relation to disability, we look for clues in how the resurrected Christ is described. After the resurrection, Jesus eats and drinks in fellowship. He has recognisable marks from the wounds of the cross, and the disciple Thomas is able to physically touch these wounds. Maja Whitaker considers the nature of these marks, whether they represent 'persisting wounds' or 'healed scars'.[257] She concludes that these marks 'may be more than merely a trace or memory of weakness or disability, but rather

---
[255] Brock (2019, xvi).
[256] Moss (2011).
[257] Whitaker (2022, 280).

the substantial embodiment of that weakness and disability in the resurrection body'.[258] Eiesland reflects on the theological significance of such a position: 'Resurrection is not about the negation or erasure of our disabled bodies in hopes of perfect images, untouched by physical disability; rather Christ's resurrection offers hope that our nonconventional, and sometimes difficult, bodies participate fully in the *imago Dei* ...'[259] Eiesland calls us to interrogate the body practices of the church, especially the Eucharist, to ensure that people with disabilities have full access to these ordinary practices (without the focus being on how disability necessitates modification).[260]

Fictional explorations of virtual reality and neural interfaces also return us to realities of embodiment and difference. In the final *Wayfarers* book, *The Galaxy, and the Ground Within* (2021), Chambers introduces 'sims' – simulated environments for virtual reality immersion. One of the characters designs sims and acknowledges the way they need to be tailored to the nervous system of the individual player. Their very design depends upon a standard bodily configuration – Chambers makes the point in relation to a marginalised species that was never mapped for sim software, but the point also hits home in relation to different and disabled human bodies.

## 5.6 What Is Flourishing?

Ultimately, engagements with technological augmentation and AI are underpinned by assumptions about what makes for a life well lived. Why do we seek 'cures' for disability (prioritising this over improving access)? What do we hope AI will achieve for us?

The science fiction examples discussed in this section are able to inspire our theological imaginations in some places, and critique them in others. Initially, the portrayal of personal robotic devices in Scalzi's work appears to be a valuable technological achievement. But reading this alongside first-hand accounts of people's lived experiences with amputation or paralysis, we are able to discern the technoableism inherent in such visions of the future. We can question why disabled individuals need to assume upright and bipedal stances in order to navigate the physical environment they share with able-bodied folks. At one point, the Haden protagonist Chris declines to use a wheelchair to compensate for a faulty personal transport unit, sourcing an expensive replacement rather than presenting physically as disabled in any way. As a wealthy Haden, Chris does not really experience disability or identify as disabled – the advantages

---

[258] Whitaker (2022, 280). For similar arguments, see also Macaskill (2019); A. Yong (2012).
[259] Eiesland (2009, 237).
[260] Eiesland (2009, 240).

of their mobility options and capabilities are emphasised and they mostly seek to be independent of any limitations posed by their biological body.[261] The fictional scenario invites us to make comparisons with disability support infrastructure and funding, and the way they are often politicised in our present world.

Siebers argues that disability 'often comes to stand for the precariousness of the human condition, for the fact that individual human beings are susceptible to change, decline over time, and die'.[262] This picture of human being is antithetical to the transhumanist endeavour, and thus disability accounts are vital in countering these particular visions of the technological future. While some within the disability community see 'enhancement' as a positive, others see it as an unwarranted and unnecessary solution.[263] Many with lived experiences of specific conditions that biotechnology is aimed at eliminating testify to the value of their 'impairments', and contend that overall human experience would be impoverished without these unique experiences.

To see technology as cure is a failure of imagination. According to Jerreat-Poole, we ought to be 'imagining uses for technology other than those animated by colonial capitalist science fiction, turning away from war, policing, productivity, and athleticism, and toward mutual care, rest, community, and collectivity'.[264] In an extended quote, they help us tie together the posthumanist emphases of the last section with the ethical imperatives of the present section's exploration of disability and technology:

> Cripping technology means envisioning an ethical relationship to technology; it means constructing relationships between organic and inorganic bodies based on mutuality, affect, interdependence, and rest. It means creating technology through non-exploitative, non-imperialist practices. It means moving away from the narrative of technological exceptionalism, in which cyborgs are superheroes who have overcome the limitations of the body. Instead, a cripped cyborg is a hybrid embodiment based on care.[265]

The imperative to create technology based on care is an immediate one. Much of the hype we have seen throughout the past few years over generative AI, whether awe-induced or anxiety-driven, has distracted us from the human labour and exploitation inherent in its history and ongoing development.[266]

---

[261] Though interestingly, Chris chooses not to completely cut off the sensory input from their body, although that is an option available with their neural network and personal transport unit connectivity.
[262] Siebers (2008, 5).
[263] Shakespeare, in Eilers, Grüber, and Rehmann-Sutter (2014, ix).
[264] Jerreat-Poole (2022, 64).
[265] Jerreat-Poole (2022, 70–71).
[266] Lorrimar (2023).

We must not allow fear or excitement over technological possibilities to prevent us from advocating for justice and equality in the here and now. Greta Byrum and Ruha Benjamin call out the 'gospel of tech solutionism', reminding us that technology on its own is not the answer to social problems. Reimagining a future with technology requires significant input from the margins if it is to genuinely address any of the issues discussed in this section, rather than merely reinforcing the status quo.[267]

We also need to think about the contexts in which action can be effective. The internet is a great connector, and has been an immense boon to many in finding groups for support, validation, and motivation. Nevertheless, Philip Butler warns against the 'sedating quality' that virtual spaces can have, a perception-distorting effect whereby 'people think their virtual social actions make concrete systemic change'.[268] Whatever form it might take, the metaverse cannot be allowed to facilitate escapism, or the equivalent of hashtag activism.[269] 'Users frequently and willingly secede the luxuries of privacy, autonomy, and personal environmental awareness in order to adhere to technology's hyper-engaging allure.'[270] Alternatively, we are duped into believing that if we only consume the *right* products, we are working to solve problems that in reality are systemic (thus cannot be addressed through individual action alone).[271]

The cripping of technology and the reimagining of a technological future that genuinely challenges the status quo is a theological task, one that substantially depends on where we locate flourishing. Together with Michael Burdett, I have elsewhere used the contrasting foci of creaturehood and deification to position some of the visions of human flourishing operating within transhumanist, secular humanist, and critical posthumanist approaches to human technological enhancement (as well as within certain theological responses).[272] We propose a theological anthropology summed up by the phrase 'creatures bound for glory' to restore a theological horizon (i.e. transcendence) to a critical posthumanist framework (as called for by Graham).[273] From a theological perspective, this makes it possible to celebrate embodiment and creaturely malleability in all the forms it takes and will take (without the need for technological cures),

---

[267] Byrum and Benjamin (2022); c.f. Boss (2022); Devenot (2023).
[268] P. Butler (2020, 5).
[269] Carr (2012).
[270] P. Butler (2020, 6).
[271] See McFarland Taylor (2019).
[272] Burdett and Lorrimar (2019). The terminology used here requires some caveats, as Jacob Boss reminds us of the plurality of transhumanisms with respect to motives and visions of flourishing (*Punks and Profiteers*).
[273] Burdett and Lorrimar (2019, 252); c.f. Graham (2004, 194).

to grapple with technological augmentation on a case-by-case basis (neither prohibition nor imperative exists), and to retain an eschatological perspective that nevertheless hopes for redemption beyond the dimensions of our present creaturely existence.

## 6 Conclusion: 'Staying with the Trouble' and Christian Hope

> Compostists eagerly found out everything they could about experimental, intentional, utopian, dystopian, and revolutionary communities and movements across times and places. One of their great disappointments in these accounts was that so many started from the premises of starting over and beginning anew, instead of learning to inherit without denial and stay with the trouble of damaged worlds. Although hardly free of the sterilizing narrative of wiping the world clean by apocalypse or salvation, the richest humus for their inquiries turned out to be SF – science fiction and fantasy, speculative fabulation, speculative feminism, and string figures. Blocking the foreclosures of utopias, SF kept politics alive.[274]

Haraway talks about 'staying with the trouble', taking up the difficult task of incremental repair without recourse to either apocalypse or salvation. The course of action rebukes techno-elitist projects of abandonment such as Elon Musk's *SpaceX* proposal to colonise Mars. It opposes certain religious notions of salvation that are also escapist – such as the 'souls in transit' understanding of human being discussed in Section 3.

Though Haraway rejects the 'premises of starting over and beginning anew', and identifies such premises with narratives of salvation, this does not make salvation unsalvageable. Arguably, staying with the trouble is precisely what a robust eschatological perspective would have us do. The promise of salvation and redemption does not get us off the hook when it comes to healing the damaged world we live in now. It may be a high-wire balancing act at times, but Christian eschatology is able to affirm the goodness, significance, and continuity of the present creation even while anticipating that God will 'make all things new' (Revelation 21:5).

### 6.1 Real-World Pathways to Fictional Utopias

What does it look like in practice to 'stay with the trouble of damaged worlds' while working towards their betterment? While science fiction can inspire us with the kinds of futures it imagines, we are left with the more pragmatic challenge of how to bring those futures to pass. This is a critique often levelled at

---

[274] Haraway (2016b, 150).

more utopian fictional works such as Chambers – they present a world that is unattainable, or at least they do not provide us with the steps to realise it.

This applies to most, if not all, visions of the future, regardless of how appealing they might be. As Boss puts it: 'Techno-utopian visions, whether of the ecomodernist sort or the cybernetic variety, often fail to take seriously the interim phase in which technologies of transformation are dependent upon uneven and unequal regimes and resources.'[275] 'You can't get there from here' is an idiom most often used in the context of giving directions to physical destinations that are difficult to reach from a current location, but it often feels true of the technofuturist visions we encounter in both science fiction and reality.

Sarah McFarland Taylor asks a similar question in relation to the 'restorying' of the world. It is all well and good, she argues, to say that we need a new story (here she is mainly referring to David Korten's contrasting of the 'sacred money and markets story' with the 'sacred life and living earth story').[276] But *how* do stories get changed, and is it even possible to have a shared cultural story any more?[277]

This question notwithstanding, McFarland Taylor explores the ways in which mediated popular culture (e.g. the depiction of the ecocity Wakanda in Marvel's *Black Panther* film) can shape real-world environmental initiatives.[278] It is a challenge, however, to bring about a 'reorientation of environmental messaging away from the notion that every tiny act counts and toward an unapologetic emphasis on broad-scale policy enactments and serious public investment'.[279] There is a real risk that popular narratives of activism can be redirected towards consumer behaviour panaceas, rather than be allowed to instigate structural change. In reading science fiction and discussing the implications for a theological imagination, we must ensure this does not remain an individual and private dream, but fuels collective action.

Nevertheless, Haraway envisions science fiction (among other SFs) as a critical source for the restorative project of healing a damaged world at the heart of *The Camille Stories*. At the same time, she does not retreat into a simplistic account of stories transforming the world merely by being shared. How might science fiction keep politics alive, and block the foreclosure of utopias, as she recounts in this fictional scenario?

A reframing of the way that we conceive of utopia might assist us with this task, and reconcile Haraway's exhortations against salvation narratives with a

---

[275] Boss (2020, 156).
[276] McFarland Taylor (2019, 19–20); c.f. Korten (2015).
[277] McFarland Taylor (2019, 20).
[278] McFarland Taylor (2019).
[279] McFarland Taylor (2019, 5).

more hopeful outlook. Kim Stanley Robinson, another science fiction writer, defines utopia in the oft-cited lines: 'Utopia is the process of making a better world, the name for one path history can take, a dynamic, tumultuous, agonizing process, with no end. Struggle forever.'[280] In other words, 'stay with the trouble'. If utopia is a process, not a final state, then we do not run the risk of foreclosing it by cementing a particular vision in place and holding it exclusively as the goal.

Such indeterminacy can make the struggle all the more difficult. When contemplating the various ills of the world we live in, and the ever encroaching crises (environmental, social, technological), despair can be a tempting way out. But as Rebecca Solnit reminds us, despair is a luxury, a response that can only belong to those cushioned from the immediate effects of climate change.[281] Instead, Solnit describes hope as the opposite of not only despair, defeatism, cynicism, or pessimism, but also optimism.[282]

Indeed, hope is central to a theological reflection on all the issues raised in this Element. A robust theological framework will also eschew the kind of retreat from the world that despair so often invokes. Richard Bauckham and Trevor Hart remind us that 'Christian hope is neither promethean nor quietist. It neither attempts what can only come from God nor neglects what is humanly possible'.[283]

Science fiction is valuable input for the Christian imagination, giving texture to hope even if it cannot itself implement the kinds of changes needed to realise the alternative worlds it projects. Jerreat-Poole describes how they look 'to science fiction and pop culture as sites to do this critical dreaming' on how augmentation technologies might be used to enact a more feminist and ethical politics into the future.[284]

In effect, this *is* what it means to 'stay with the trouble' as theologians and scholars. Story may not be everything, but it is nevertheless the medium that theologians and philosophers work with. Not quite in the sense that Haraway envisions, perhaps, as a Christian hope does look to divine salvation after all. But also not in a way that belies the urgency of acting in the present.

At the very least, we must ensure that our theological frameworks do not discourage the kind of initiatives required to enact real world change. N.T. Wright admits that he does not know exactly how the present and new creation are related (the new creation is at the same time continuous and discontinuous

---

[280] Robinson (1990, 95).
[281] Solnit (17 July 2023).
[282] Solnit (17 July 2023). This is reminiscent of Eagleton (2015).
[283] Bauckham and Hart (1999, 41).
[284] Jerreat-Poole (2022, 61).

with the present, but *how* exactly is beyond our knowledge). He assures us with conviction, however that working to heal the present world is building the kingdom of God. 'What you *do* in the present – by painting, preaching, singing, sewing, praying, teaching, building hospitals, digging wells, campaigning for justice, writing poems, caring for the needy, loving your neighbour as yourself – all these things *will last into God's future.*'[285]

Drawing inspiration from the imagined worlds constructed by authors of science fiction (whom Christina Bieber Lake designates as 'prophets of the posthuman'),[286] a theological approach to human being in relation to emerging technologies such as artificial intelligence and mind-uploading can sustain hope without foreclosing utopia. It may be enriched by posthumanist scholarship and disability theory inflected in explicitly theological interpretations to ensure that the future is not imagined for the edification of a narrow slice of humanity. It might incorporate a deep incarnational perspective that does not privilege human uniqueness in determining what future flourishing could look like.

This Element remains a theoretical work, rather than a political manifesto or action plan. By and large, theologians are not the ones doing the practical work of healing a damaged world. Most of us are not developing and implementing technologies, or writing policy and passing legislation, or providing essential services to those laid low by exploitative practices, war, or natural disaster. But many of us are engaged in the kind of theological reflection that (hopefully) trickles down from academic symposia and outputs into textbooks and pulpits, and influences those who minister to and teach and care for many more. Let us not think of our contribution more highly than we ought.

So I conclude on a rather ambivalent note, fitting given the tensions inherent to staying with the trouble. Yes, the imaginings that shape our theological understanding and convictions matter, and we do well to read widely and draw on science fiction in our reflection around the future of creation with technology. No, a good story is not enough on its own to bring about the degree of healing required, especially if that story envisions a utopia installed by wiping the slate clean. We are responsible to act as well as to imagine. We do both out of hope.

---

[285] Wright (2004, 205), emphasis original.
[286] Bieber Lake (2013).

# References

Ali, S. M. (2019). 'White Crisis' and/as 'existential risk,' or the entangled apocalypticism of artificial intelligence. *Zygon*, *54*(1), 207–224.

Allan, K. (Ed.). (2013). *Disability in science fiction: Representations of technology as cure*. New York: Palgrave Macmillan.

Axelrod, J. B. C. (2018). Mutiny on the sofa: Historical patterns of patriarchy and family structure in American science fiction, 1945–2018. *Pacific Coast Philology*, *53*(2), 308–334.

Bacon, F. (1964). The masculine birth of time. In B. Farrington (Ed.), *The philosophy of Francis Bacon: An essay on its development from 1603–1609* (pp. 59-72). Liverpool: Liverpool University Press.

Barrera, A. (2005). *Economic compulsion and Christian ethics*. Cambridge: Cambridge University Press.

Bauckham, R., & Hart, T. (1999). *Hope against hope: Christian eschatology at the turn of the millennium*. Grand Rapids, MI: Eerdmans.

Beckert, J. (2016). *Imagined futures: Fictional expectations and capitalist dynamics*. Cambridge, MA: Harvard University Press.

Bieber Lake, C. (2013). *Prophets of the posthuman: American fiction, biotechnology, and the ethics of personhood*. Notre Dame, IN: University of Notre Dame Press.

Bly, R. (2005). *The science in science fiction: Eighty-three SF predictions that became scientific reality*. Dallas, TX: BenBella.

Boellstorff, T. (2015). *Coming of age in second life: An anthropologist explores the virtually human*. Princeton, NJ: Princeton University Press.

Booker, M. K., & Thomas, A.-M. (2009). *The science fiction handbook*. Chichester: Wiley-Blackwell.

Boss, J. (2020). The harmony of metal and flesh: Cybernetic futures. In C. Hrynkow (Ed.), *Spiritualities, ethics, and implications of human enhancement and artificial intelligence* (pp. 139–157). Wilmington, DE: Vernon Press.

Boss, J. (2022). Punks and profiteers in the war on death. *Body and Religion*, online first. https://doi.org/10.1558/bar.18251.

Bostrom, N. (2003). The transhumanist FAQ: A general introduction (version 2.1). *World Transhumanist Association*. www.nickbostrom.com/views/transhumanist.pdf.

Bostrom, N. (2005). A history of transhumanist thought. *Journal of Evolution and Technology*, *14*(1), 1–27.

Bostrom, N. (2008). Letter from utopia. *Ethics, Law and Technology*, *2*(1), 1–7.
Braidotti, R. (2013). *The posthuman*. Cambridge: Polity Press.
Brake, M., & Hook, N. (2008). *Different engines: How science drives fiction and fiction drives science*. London: Macmillan.
Brock, B. (2019). *Wondrously wounded: Theology, disability, and the body of Christ*. Waco, TX: Baylor University Press.
Brotherton, M. (Ed.). (2017). *Science fiction by scientists: An anthology of short stories*. Cham: Springer.
Bujić, M., Salminen, M., Macey, J., & Hamari, J. (2020). 'Empathy machine': How virtual reality affects human rights attitudes. *Internet Research*, *30*(5), 1407–1425. https://doi.org/10.1108/intr-07-2019-0306.
Burdett, M. (2017). Assessing the field of science and religion: Advice from the next generation. *Zygon*, *52*(3), 747–763.
Burdett, M., & Leung, K.-H. (2023). The machine in the ghost: Transhumanism and the ontology of information. *Zygon*, *48*(3), 714–731. https://doi.org/10.1111/zygo.12886.
Burdett, M., & Lorrimar, V. (2019). Creatures bound for glory: Biotechnological enhancement and visions of human flourishing. *Studies in Christian Ethics*, *32*(2), 241–253.
Butler, O. (1987). *Dawn*. New York, NY: Grand Central.
Butler, P. (2020). *Black transhuman liberation theology*. London: Bloomsbury.
Byrum, G., & Benjamin, R. (2022). Disrupting the gospel of tech solutionism to build tech justice. *Stanford Social Innovation Review*. https://ssir.org/articles/entry/disrupting_the_gospel_of_tech_solutionism_to_build_tech_justice#.
Calloway, K., & Strawn, B. (2020). Experimental theology: Theological anthropology and the psychological sciences. *Journal of Psychology and Theology*, *48*(1), 3–17.
Carr, D. (2012). Hashtag activism and its limits. *The New York Times*, 25 March. www.nytimes.com/2012/03/26/business/media/hashtag-activism-and-its-limits.html.
Chalmers, D. (2010). The singularity: A philosophical analysis. *Journal of Consciousness Studies*, *17*, 7–65.
Chambers, B. (2015). *The long way to a small, angry planet*. London: Hodder & Stoughton.
Chambers, B. (2016). *A closed and common orbit*. London: Hodder & Stoughton.
Chambers, B. (2019). *Record of a spaceborn few*. London: Hodder & Stoughton.
Chambers, B. (2021a). *The galaxy, and the ground within*. London: Hodder & Stoughton.

Chambers, B. (2021b). *A psalm for the wild-built*. New York: Tor Books.

Chambers, B. (2022). *A prayer for the crown-shy*. New York, NY: Tor Books.

Cheng, S. (2023). *Metaverse: Concept, content and context*. Cham: Springer.

Chu, S.-Y. (2010). *Do metaphors dream of literal sheep? A science-fictional theory of representation*. Cambridge, MA: Harvard University Press.

Clark, A. (1997). *Being there: Putting brain, body, and world together again*. Cambridge, MA: MIT Press.

Cline, E. (2011). *Ready player one*. New York, NY: Random House.

Cline, E. (2020). *Ready player two*. New York, NY: Random House.

Clough, D. (2013). *On animals*. London: Bloomsbury.

Cortez, M. (2010). *Theological anthropology: A guide for the perplexed*. London: T & T Clark.

Cotton, M. (2021). *Virtual reality, empathy and ethics*. London: Palgrave McMillan.

Davis, L. (2006). Constructing normalcy: the bell curve, the novel, and the invention of the disabled body in the nineteenth century. In L. Davis (Ed.). *The disability studies reader*. New York, NY: Routledge.

Davies, P. (27 April 2016). Putting the science in fiction. *Cosmos*. https://cosmosmagazine.com/the-future/putting-science-fiction.

Davison, A. (2021). Machine learning and theological traditions of analogy. *Modern Theology, 37*(2), 254–274.

Dery, M. (1999). *The pyrotechnic insanitarium: American culture on the brink*. New York: Grove Press.

Devenot, N. (2023). TESCREAL hallucinations: Psychedelic and AI hype as inequality engines. *Journal of Psychedelic Studies, Online first*. https://doi.org/10.1556/2054.2023.00292

Disch, T. (1998). *The Dreams Our Stuff Is Made Of: How Science Fiction Conquered the World*. New York: Simon & Schuster.

Doctorow, C. (2017). I've created a monster! (and so can you). In D. Guston, E. Finn, & J. Robert (Eds.), *Frankenstein, or the modern Prometheus: Annotated for scientists, engineers, and creators of all kinds* (pp. 209–213). Cambridge, MA: MIT Press.

Doctorow, C., & Stross, C. (2012). *The rapture of the nerds*. New York, NY: Tor Books.

Eagleton, T. (2015). *Hope without optimism*. New Haven, CT: Yale University Press.

Eiesland, N. (1994). *The disabled God: Toward a liberatory theology of disability*. Nashville, TN: Abingdon Press.

Eiesland, N. (2009). Sacramental bodies. *Journal of Religion, Disability and Health, 13*(3–4), 236–246.

# References

Eilers, M., Grüber, K., & Rehmann-Sutter, C. (Eds.). (2014). *The human enhancement debate and disability: New bodies for a better life*. Basingstoke: Palgrave Macmillan.

Ellcessor, E. (2016). *Restricted access: Media, disability, and the politics of participation*. New York, NY: New York University Press.

Ellul, J. (1980). *The technological system* (J. Neugroschel, Trans.). New York: Continuum.

Ewart, C. (2019). An arm up or a leg down? grounding the prosthesis and other instabilities. In D. Mitchell, S. Antebi, & S. Snyder (Eds.), *The matter of disability: Materiality, biopolitics, crip affect* (pp. 160–181). Ann Arbor, MI: University of Michigan Press.

Francis. (2015). *Laudato si'*. Rome: Vatican.

Fuller, M. (Ed.). (2022). *Science and religion in Western literature: Critical and theological studies*. London: Routledge.

Geraci, R. (2010). *Apocalyptic AI: Visions of heaven in robotics, artificial intelligence, and virtual reality*. New York: Oxford University Press.

Gibson, W. (1984). *Neuromancer*. New York: Ace Books.

Gigerenzer, G. and Goldstein, D. (1996). Mind as computer: birth of a metaphor. *Creativity Research Journal, 9*(2), 131–144.

Goode, L. (2019). Singularity. In H. Paul (Ed.), *Critical terms in future studies* (pp. 281–286). Cham: Palgrave Macmillan.

Goodley, D., & Runswick-Cole, K. (2016). Becoming dishuman: Thinking about the human through dis/ability. *Discourse: Studies in the Cultural Politics of Education, 37*(1), 1–15.

Graham, E. (2002a). Nietzsche gets a modem: Transhumanism and the technological sublime. *Literature and Theology, 16*(1), 65–80.

Graham, E. (2002b). *Representations of the posthuman: Monsters, aliens and others in popular culture*. New Brunswick, NJ: Rutgers University Press.

Graham, E. (2004). Bioethics after posthumanism: Natural law, communicative action and the problem of self-design. *Ecotheology, 9*(2), 178–198.

Graham, E. (2006). In whose image? Representations of technology and the 'ends' of humanity. *Ecotheology, 11*(2), 159–182.

Green, S. E., & Loseke, D. R. (Eds.). (2020). *New narratives of disability: Constructions, clashes, and controversies*. Belford: Emerald.

Gregerson, N. H. (2001). The cross of Christ in an evolutionary world. *Dialog: A Journal of Theology, 40*, 192–207.

Grillmayr, J. (2019). Posthumanism(s). In A. McFarlane, L. Schmeink, & G. Murphy (Eds.), *The Routledge companion to cyberpunk culture* (pp. 273–281). London: Routledge.

Gunn, E. (May 2014). How America's leading science fiction authors are shaping your future. *Smithsonian Magazine.* www.smithsonianmag.com/arts-culture/how-americas-leading-science-fiction-authors-are-shaping-your-future-180951169/.

Hamraie, A., & Fritsch, K. (2019, April). Crip technoscience manifesto. *Catalyst: Feminism, Theory, Technoscience, 5*(1), 1–33. http://dx.doi.org/10.28968/cftt.v5i1.29607 https://doi.org/10.28968/cftt.v5i1.29607.

Haraway, D. (1991). A cyborg manifesto: Science, technology, and socialist-feminism in the late twentieth century. In *Simians, cyborgs and women: The reinvention of nature* (pp. 149–181). New York: Routledge.

Haraway, D. (1992). Ecce homo, ain't (ar'n't) I a woman, and inappropriate/d others: The human in a post-humanist landscape. In J. Butler & J. Scott (Eds.), *Feminists theorize the political* (pp. 86–100). New York, NY: Routledge.

Haraway, D. (2008). *When species meet.* Minneapolis, MN: University of Minnesota Press.

Haraway, D. (2016a). *Manifestly Haraway.* Minneapolis, MN: University of Minnesota Press.

Haraway, D. (2016b). *Staying with the trouble: Making kin in the Chthulucene.* Minneapolis, MN: Duke University Press.

Harrison, P., & Milbank, J. (2022). *After science and religion: Fresh perspectives from philosophy and theology.* Cambridge: Cambridge University Press.

Harrison, P., & Tyson, P. (2022). *New directions in theology and science: beyond dialogue.* London: Routledge.

Hayles, N. K. (1999). *How we became posthuman: Virtual bodies in cybernetics, literature, and informatics.* Chicago, IL: University of Chicago Press.

Hayles, N. K. (2012). *How we think: Digital media and contemporary technogenesis.* Chicago, IL: University of Chicago Press.

Heinlein, R. (2017). On the writing of speculative fiction. In R. Latham (Ed.), *Science fiction criticism: An anthology of essential writings* (pp. 17–21). New York, NY: Bloomsbury Academic.

Herbrechter, S. (2018). Critical posthumanism. In R. Braidotti & M. Hlavajova (Eds.), *Posthuman glossary* (pp. 94–96). London: Bloomsbury.

Herzfeld, N. (2016). More than information: A Christian critique of a new dualism. *Theology and Science, 14*(1), 84–92. https://doi.org/0.1080/14746700.2015.1122337.

Herzfeld, N. (2023). *The artifice of intelligence: Divine and human relationship in a robotic age.* Minneapolis, MN: Fortress Press.

Hobbes, T. (1958). *Leviathan*. New York, NY: Library of Liberal Arts.
Hoffman, M., & Pfeifer, R. (2012). The implications of embodiment for behavior and cognition: Animal and robotic case studies. In W. Tschacher & C. Bergomi (Eds.), *The implications of embodiment: Cognition and communication* (pp. 31–58). Exeter: Imprint Academic.
Hopkinson, N. (2003). Nalo Hopkinson: Fantasy island girl. In D. Bailey Nurse (Ed.), *What's a black critic to do?: Interviews, profiles and reviews of black writers* (pp. 139–145). Toronto, CA: Insomniac Press.
Hrotic, S. (2016). *Religion in science fiction: The evolution of an idea and the extinction of a genre*. London: Bloomsbury.
Imfeld, Z. L. (2021). Have we forgotten how to have fun in 'literature and science'? *Anglistik*, *32*(3), 121–134. https://doi.org/10.33675/ANGL/2021/3/11.
Jasanoff, S. (2017). A field of its own: The emergence of science and technology studies. In *The Oxford handbook of interdisciplinarity* (pp. 173–187). Oxford: Oxford University Press. https://doi.org/10.1093/oxfordhb/9780198733522.013.15.
Jerreat-Poole, A. (2022). Virtual reality, disability, and futurity: Cripping technologies in *Half-Life: Alyx*. *Journal of Literary & Cultural Disability Studies*, *16*(1), 59–75.
Johnson, E. (2014). *Ask the beasts: Darwin and the God of love*. London: Bloomsbury.
Johnson, M. (1993). *Moral imagination: Implications of cognitive science for ethics*. Chicago, IL: University of Chicago Press.
Jonsson, E. (2021). *The early evolutionary imagination: Literature and human nature*. Cham: Palgrave Macmillan.
Kafer, A. (2013). *Feminist, queer, crip*. Bloomington, IN: Indiana University Press.
Kelsey, D. (2002). Spiritual machines, personal bodies, and God: Theological education and theological anthropology. *Teaching Theology & Religion*, *5*(1), 2–9. https://doi.org/10.1111/1467-9647.00112.
Kelsey, D. (2009). *Eccentric existence: A theological anthropology* (Vol. 1). Louisville, KY: Westminster John Knox Press.
Korten, D. (2015). *Change the story, change the future: A living ecology for a living earth*. Oakland, CA: Berrett-Koehler.
Kull, A. (2001). Cyborg embodiment and the incarnation. *Currents in Theology and Mission*, *28*(3–4), 279–284.
Kurzweil, R. (2005). *The Singularity is near: When humans transcend biology*. London: Penguin Books.

Kwok, P.- l. (2005). *Postcolonial imagination and feminist theology*. London: SCM Press.

Lakoff, G., & Johnson, M. (2003). *Metaphors we live by*. Chicago, IL: University of Chicago Press. (Original work published 1980).

Le Guin, U. (1973). On Norman Spinrad's 'the iron dream.' *Science Fiction Studies*, *1*(1), 41–44.

Le Guin, U. (1989). Is gender necessary? Redux (1976/1987). In *Dancing at the end of the world: Thoughts on words, women, places* (pp. 7–16). New York, NY: Grove Press.

Lorrimar, V. (2019). Mind uploading and embodied cognition: A theological response. *Zygon: Journal of Religion and Science*, *54*(1), 191–206.

Lorrimar, V. (2020). Science and religion: Moving beyond the credibility strategy. *Zygon*, *55*(3), 812–823.

Lorrimar, V. (2022a). *Human technological enhancement and theological anthropology*. Cambridge, UK: Cambridge University Press.

Lorrimar, V. (2022b). Imagining human futures: Co-creation and technological enhancement. In B. Sollereder & A. McGrath (Eds.), *Emerging voices in science and religion: Contributions from young women*. London: Routledge.

Lorrimar, V. (2023). Going beyond the anxiety-awe spectrum by putting the human back into artificial intelligence. *American Religion*, *5*(1), 111–117.

Lorrimar, V. (2025, forthcoming). Theological anthropology. In C. McKirland (Ed.), *The T & T clark encyclopedia of Christian doctrine*. London: T & T Clark.

Macaskill, G. (2019). *Autism and the church: A biblical and theological study*. Waco, TX: Baylor University Press.

Maienschein, J., & MacCord, K. (2017). Changing conceptions of human nature. In D. Guston, E. Finn, & J. Robert (Eds.), *Frankenstein, or the modern Prometheus: Annotated for scientists, engineers, and creators of all kinds* (pp. 217–228). Cambridge, MA: MIT Press.

Mann, J. (2018). Pessimistic futurism: Survival and reproduction in Octavia Butler's *Dawn*. *Feminist Theory*, *19*(1), 61–76.

McFarland Taylor, S. (2019). *Ecopiety: Green media and the dilemma of environmental virtue*. New York, NY: New York University Press.

McFarlane, A., Schmeink, L., & Murphy, G. (2019). Cyberpunk as cultural formation. In A. McFarlane, L. Schmeink, & G. Murphy (Eds.), *The Routledge companion to cyberpunk culture* (pp. 1–3). London: Routledge.

McGilchrist, I. (2009). *The Master and His Emissary: The Divided Brain and the Making of the Western World*. New Haven, CT: Yale University Press.

Mendlesohn, F. (2003). Religion and science fiction. In E. James (Ed.), *The Cambridge companion to science fiction* (pp. 264–275). Cambridge: Cambridge University Press.

Merril, J. (2017). What do you mean: Science? Fiction? In R. Latham (Ed.), *Science fiction criticism: An anthology of essential writings* (pp. 22–36). New York, NY: Bloomsbury Academic.

Midson, S. (2018). *Cyborg theology: Humans, technology and God.* London: I. B. Taurus.

Midson, S. and O'Donnell, K. (2020). Rethinking relationships in cyberspace. *Theology & Sexuality, 26*(2–3), 83–98.

Milburn, C. (2010). Modifiable futures: Science fiction at the bench. *Isis, 101*, 560–569.

Milburn, C. (2014). Posthumanism. In R. Latham (Ed.), *The Oxford handbook of science fiction* (pp. 524–536). Oxford: Oxford University Press.

Miller, C., & Bennett, I. (2008). Thinking longer term about technology: Is there value in science fiction-inspired approaches to constructing futures. *Science and Public Policy, 35*(8), 597–606.

Moor, J. (2006). The Dartmouth College artificial intelligence conference: The next fifty years. *AI Magazine, 27*(4), 87. https://ojs.aaai.org/aimagazine/index.php/aimagazine/article/view/1911 https://doi.org/10.1609/aimag.v27i4.1911.

Moravec, H. (1988). *Mind children: The future of robot and human intelligence.* Cambridge, MA: Harvard University Press.

Moss, C. R. (2011). Heavenly healing: Eschatological cleansing and the resurrection of the dead in the early church. *Journal of the American Academy of Religion, 79*(4), 991–1017.

Ni, Z. (2020). Reimagining Daoist alchemy, decolonizing transhumanism: The fantasy of immortality cultivation in twenty-first century China. *Zygon, 55*(3), 748–771.

Nussbaum, M. (1990). Transcending humanity. In *Love's knowledge: Essays on philosophy and literature* (pp. 365–392). New York: Oxford University Press.

O'Gieblyn, M. (18 April 2017). God in the machine: My strange journey into transhumanism. *The Guardian.* www.theguardian.com/technology/2017/apr/18/god-in-the-machine-my-strange-journey-into-transhumanism.

Pecchenino, R. (2007). On tanner's 'economy of grace': An economist responds. *Irish Theological Quarterly, 72*, 96–104.

Perry, J., & Leidenhag, J. (2023). *Science-engaged theology.* Cambridge: Cambridge University Press.

Persson, I., & Savulescu, J. (2012). *Unfit for the future: The need for moral enhancement*. Oxford: Oxford University Press.

Pesce, M. (October 1999). Magic mirror: The novel as a software development platform. *MIT Communications Forum*. http://web.mit.edu/comm-forum/papers/pesce.html.

Pico della Mirandola, G. (1956). *Oration on the dignity of man* (A. R. Caponigri, Trans.). Chicago, IL: Henry Regnery Co.

Piette, J. D., Newman, S., Krein, S. L. et al. (2022). Artificial intelligence (AI) to improve chronic pain care: Evidence of AI learning. *Intelligence-Based Medicine*, *6*, 100064. www.sciencedirect.com/science/article/pii/S2666521222000175 https://doi.org/10.1016/j.ibmed.2022.100064

Quayson, A. (2007). *Aesthetic nervousness: Disability and the crisis of representation*. New York: Columbia University Press.

Raulerson, J. (2013). *Singularities: Technoculture, transhumanism, and science fiction in the 21st century*. Liverpool: Liverpool University Press.

Reeves, J. (2019). *Against methodology in science and religion: Recent debates on rationality and theology*. London: Routledge.

Reeves, J. (2020). Methodology in science and religion - a reply to critics. *Zygon: Journal of Religion and Science*, *55*(3), 824–836.

Robinson, K. S. (1990). *Pacific edge*. London: HarperCollins.

Roldán Romero, V. (2022). Transhumanism and the Anthropocene in Becky Chamber's *A Closed and Common Orbit*. *Revista de Estudios Norteamericanos*, *26*. https://revistascientificas.us.es/index.php/ESTUDIOS_NORTEAMERICANOS/article/view/18023 https://doi.org/10.12795/REN.2022.i26.04

Sawyer, R. (2005). *Mindscan*. New York: Tor.

Scalzi, J. (2014a). *Lock in*. London: Tor Books.

Scalzi, J. (2014b). *Unlocked: An oral history of Haden's syndrome*. Tor Books. www.tor.com/2014/05/13/unlocked-an-oral-history-of-hadens-syndrome-john-scalzi/.

Scalzi, J. (2020). *Head on*. London: Tor Books.

Schalk, S. (2020). Wounded warriors of the future: Disability hierarchy in *Avatar* and *Source Code*. *Journal of Literary & Cultural Disability Studies*, *14*(4), 403–419.

Scott, P. A. (1997). Imagination in practice. *Journal of Medical Ethics*, *23*(1), 45–50.

Seed, D. (2011). *Science fiction: A very short introduction*. Oxford: Oxford University Press.

Selke, L., & al Ayad, D. (Eds.). (2012). *Outlaw bodies: A speculative fiction anthology*. Futurefire.net.

Shatner, W., & Walter, C. (2002). *I'm working on that: A trek from science fiction to science fact*. New York: Pocket.

Shew, A. (2023). *Against technoableism: Rethinking who needs improvement*. New York, NY: W. W. Norton.

Siebers, T. (2008). *Disability theory*. Ann Arbor, MI: University of Michigan Press.

Singler, B. (2022). Left behind? Religion as a vestige in 'The Rapture of the Nerds' and other AI singularity literature. In M. Fuller (Ed.), *Science and religion in western literature: Critical and theological studies* (pp. 136–150). London: Routledge.

Smedes, T. (2008). Beyond Barbour or back to basics? The future of science-and-religion and the quest for unity. *Zygon, 43*(1), 235–258.

Smith, J. K. (2022). *Robot theology: Old questions through new media*. Eugene, OR: Resource.

Smith, J. K. A. (2009). *Desiring the kingdom: Worship, worldview, and cultural formation*. Grand Rapids, MI: Baker Academic.

Snow, C. P. (1961). *The two cultures and the scientific revolution*. Cambridge: Cambridge University Press. (Original work published 1961).

Solana, M. (14 August 2014). Stop writing dystopian sci-fi: It's making us all fear technology. *Wired*. www.wired.com/2014/08/stop-writing-dystopian-sci-fiits-making-us-all-fear-technology/.

Sollereder, B. (2019). *God, evolution, and animal suffering: Theodicy without a fall*. London: Routledge.

Solnit, R. (17 July 2023). Why climate despair is a luxury. *The New Statesman*. www.newstatesman.com/environment/2023/07/rebecca-solnit-climate-pair-hope.

Southgate, C. (2008). *The groaning of creation: God, evolution and the problem of evil*. Louisville, KY: Westminster John Knox Press.

Spivak, G. C., & Morris, R. C. (2010). *Can the subaltern speak? Reflections on the history of an idea*. New York: Columbia University Press.

Stainforth, E., & Walton, J. L. (2019). Computing utopia: The horizons of computational economies in history and science fiction. *Science Fiction Studies, 46*(3), 471–489. http://dx.doi.org/10.1353/sfs.2019.0084 https://doi.org/10.1353/sfs.2019.0084.

Stallman, R. (2012). *Made for you*. Retrieved 2018-03-10, from https://ieet.org/index.php/IEET2/more/stallman20121228.

Star, S. (1991). Power, technology and the phenomenology of conventions: On being allergic to onions. In J. Law (Ed.), *A sociology of monsters: Essays on power, technology and domination* (pp. 25–56). London: Routledge.

Stephenson, N. (1992). *Snow crash*. New York, NY: Bantam Books.

Stephenson, N. (2019). *Fall; or, dodge in hell*. New York, NY: William Morrow.
Stephenson, N. (2021). *Termination shock*. New York, NY: HarperCollins.
Stross, C. (2004). *The family trade*. New York, NY: Tor Books.
Stross, C. (2006). *Glasshouse* (electronic ed.). London: Berkley Publishing Group.
Stross, C. (2018). *Dark state*. New York, NY: Tor Books.
Szerszynski, B. (2005). *Nature, technology and the sacred*. Oxford: Blackwell Publishing.
Tanner, K. (2005). *Economy of grace*. Minneapolis, MN: Fortress Press.
Tanner, K. (2009). *Christ the key*. Cambridge: Cambridge University Press.
Tanton, T. (2023). *Corporeal theology: The nature of theological understanding in light of embodied cognition*. Oxford: Oxford University Press.
Tassinari, M., Aulbach, M. B., & Jasinskaja-Lahti, I. (2022, February). Investigating the influence of intergroup contact in virtual reality on empathy: An exploratory study using altspacevr. *Frontiers in Psychology, 12*. http://dx.doi.org/10.3389/fpsyg.2021.815497, https://doi.org/10.3389/fpsyg.2021.815497.
Terrone, E. (2021). Science fiction as genre. *The Journal of Aesthetics and Art Criticism, 79*, 16–19. https://doi.org/10.1093/jaac/kpaa003.
Thorstad, D. (2024). Against the singularity hypothesis. *Philosophical Studies*. https://doi.org/10.1007/s11098-024-02143-5.
Thweatt-Bates, J. (2012). *Cyborg selves: A theological anthropology of the posthuman*. Surrey: Ashgate.
Tiptree, J., Jr. (2004). The girl who was plugged in. In *Her smoke rose up forever* (pp. 43–78). San Francisco, CA: Tachyon. (Original work published 1973).
van der Kolk, B. (2014). *The body keeps the score: Brain, mind, and body in the healing of trauma*. London: Penguin.
van der Laan, J. M. (2010). Frankenstein as Science Fiction and Fact. *Bulletin of Science, Technology & Society, 30*(4), 298–304.
Vinge, V. (1986). *Marooned in realtime*. New York, NY: Blue Jay.
Vint, S. (2007). *Bodies of tomorrow: Technology, subjectivity, science fiction*. Toronto: University of Toronto Press.
Voss Roberts, M. (2017). *Body parts: A theological anthropology*. Minneapolis, MN: Fortress Press.
Waters, B. (2006). *From human to posthuman: Christian theology and technology in a postmodern world*. Aldershot: Ashgate.
Weise, J. (2020). Common cyborg. In A. Wong (Ed.), *Disability visibility: First-person stories from the twenty-first century* (pp. 63–74). London: Vintage Books.

Westfahl, G., & Slusser, G. (Eds.). (2009). *Science fiction and the two cultures: Essays on bridging the gap between the sciences and the humanities*. Jefferson, NC: McFarland.

Whitaker, M. (2022). The wounds of the risen Christ: Evidence for the retention of disabling conditions in the resurrection body. *Journal of Disability & Religion, 26*(3), 280–293.

White Jr, L. (1967). The historical roots of our ecologic crisis. *Science, 155*, 1203–1207.

Wilding, C., Young, K., Cummins, C., et al. (2022, October). Virtual reality to foster empathy in disability workers: A feasibility study during COVID-19. *Journal of Applied Research in Intellectual Disabilities, 36*(1), 132–142. https://doi.org/10.1111/jar.13042.

Wilhelm, A. (2023, November). Effective accelerationism, doomers, decels, and how to flaunt your ai priors. *TechCrunch*. https://techcrunch.com/2023/11/20/e-acc-doomers-decels-openai-altman/.

Willems, B. (2020). Speculative realism: The human and nonhuman divide. In S. Vint (Ed.), *After the human: Culture, theory, and criticism in the 21st century* (pp. 92–205). Cambridge: Cambridge University Press.

Williams, D. (2019). Heavenly bodies: Why it matters that cyborgs have always been about disability, mental health, and marginalization. *SSRN*. http://dx.doi.org/10.2139/ssrn.3401342.

Wittgenstein, L. (1960). *Tractatus logico-philosophicus*. London: Routledge.

Wolfe, C. (2010). *What is posthumanism?* Minneapolis, MN: University of Minnesota Press.

Womack, Y. (2013). *Afrofuturism: The world of black sci-fi and fantasy culture*. Chicago, IL: Chicago Review Press.

Wright, N. T. (2004). *Surprised by hope: Rethinking heaven, the resurrection, and the mission of the church*. London: HarperCollins.

Wright, N. T., & Borg, M. (1999). *The meaning of Jesus*. London: SPCK.

Wynter, S. (2003). Unsettling the coloniality of being/power/truth/freedom: Towards the human, after man, its overrepresentation – an argument. *CR: The New Centennial Review, 3*(3), 257–337.

Yong, A. (2012). Disability theology of the resurrection: Persisting questions and additional considerations – a response to Ryan Mullins. *Ars Disputandi, 12*(1), 4–10. https://doi.org/10.1080/15665399.2012.10820066.

Yong, E. (2022). *An immense world: How animal senses reveal the hidden realms around us*. London: Random House.

Zhou, M., Leenders, M. A., & Cong, L. M. (2018). Ownership in the virtual world and the implications for long-term user innovation success. *Technovation, 78*, 56–65.

# Acknowledgements

In 2019 I was invited to take part in a panel at the American Academy of Religion (AAR) annual meeting responding to Joshua Reeves' *Against Methodology in Science and Religion* (2020). This gave me an opportunity to situate my thinking about science fiction and its value for theology within the broader methodological debates of the science and religion field, and I am grateful to both Reeves and to Paul Allen for convening the panel, and to Michael Burdett for presenting my paper in my stead. I also benefitted from the questions and discussion in response to papers I presented in sessions sponsored by the Religion and Science Fiction program unit at the AAR annual meetings in 2017 and 2020. Thanks also go to members of the Human Augmentation Research Network and to Nika Hiraeth for providing feedback on an incomplete draft of this work.

## Cambridge Elements

# Christianity and Science

### Andrew Davison
*University of Cambridge*

Andrew Davison is the Starbridge Associate Professor in Theology and Science at the University of Cambridge. He is Fellow of Corpus Christi College and Dean of the Chapel, and looks after the arts and humanities work of the Leverhulme Centre for Life in the Universe at the University of Cambridge.

### Editorial Board

Natalie Carnes, *Baylor University*

Helen de Cruz, *St. Louis University*

Peter Harrison, *University of Queensland*

Sarah Lane Ritchie, *John Templeton Foundation*

Lisa Sideris, *University of California, Santa Barbara*

Jacob Sherman, *California Institute of Integral Studies*

Ignacio Alberto Silva, *Universidad Austral, Argentina*

### About the Series

The Elements series on Christianity and Science will offer an authoritative presentation of scholarship in this interdisciplinary field of inquiry. Opening new avenues for study and research, the series will highlight several issues, notably the importance of historical scholarship for understanding the relationship between Christianity and natural science, and the vital role played by philosophy in this field today.

Cambridge Elements =

# Christianity and Science

## Elements in the Series

*Eastern Orthodoxy and the Science-Theology Dialogue*
Christopher C. Knight

*Science-Engaged Theology*
John Perry and Joanna Leidenhag

*Science Fiction and Christian Theology*
Victoria Lorrimar

A full series listing is available at: www.cambridge.org/EOCS

For EU product safety concerns, contact us at Calle de José Abascal, 56–1°,
28003 Madrid, Spain or eugpsr@cambridge.org.